Handling Diversity in the Workplace:
Communication Is the Key

Kay duPont, CSP
Foreword by Dr. R. Roosevelt Thomas

American Media Publishing
4900 University Avenue
West Des Moines, Iowa 50266-6769
800/262-2557

Handling Diversity in the Workplace: Communication Is the Key

Kay duPont, CSP
Copyright 1997 by American Media Incorporated

Credits:
American Media Publishing: Arthur Bauer
                              Todd McDonald
Managing Editor: Karen Massetti Miller
Layout and Design: Gayle O'Brien
Cover Design: Polly Beaver

Published by American Media Inc.
4900 University Avenue
West Des Moines, IA 50266-6769

Library of Congress Card Number 96-080413
duPont, Kay
Handling Diversity in the Workplace: Communication Is the Key

Printed in the United States of America
1997
ISBN 1-884926-72-X

About the Author

Kay duPont is recognized as one of America's foremost speakers and trainers in human communication and relationships. Her expertise extends to interpersonal skills, business writing, public speaking and presentation skills, teamwork and diversity, and relationship building.

Her ability to assess her clients' and readers' needs, quickly establish rapport, and present solutions in a humorous, interactive way are the keys to her success. Her books and training programs help people communicate more effectively, create better impressions, and remove obstacles to better performance.

Kay is owner and executive vice president of The Communication Connection, an Atlanta-based company that offers consulting, training courses, and speeches in business relationships, image, and communication. Kay started writing at the age of six and is the author of four other books as well as several audio and video programs.

Kay also holds the Certified Speaking Professional designation, which ranks her in the top 7 percent of the world's speakers, and she has been named by *Successful Meetings* magazine as one of the country's top female presenters. In addition, she has won many speaking, training, writing, and community service awards for her outstanding work. She is a member of the National Speakers Association, the Georgia Speakers Association, and the American Society for Training and Development. She also serves as a volunteer coordinator for Habitat for Humanity.

For more information, contact American Media Incorporated or The Communication Connection, 2137 Mount Vernon Road, Atlanta, Georgia 30338.

Introduction

As the U.S. population has become increasingly diverse, so has the U.S. workplace. The federal government's Workforce 2000 study and the Census Bureau assure us that these population changes will continue for many years.

To succeed in our multicultural society, your organization must value the differences of our diverse population, respect the individuality of all employees and customers, and maintain a climate in which everyone is treated with dignity. To do this, you need to understand the current demographics of America and its businesses and anticipate tomorrow's population. You also need to understand how your words and actions in today's diverse workplace and marketplace affect your bottom line, and you need to maintain and exhibit a positive outlook on diversity.

Everyone in business today needs to better understand other cultures, as well as other age groups, gender groups, and lifestyle groups. We also need to be acutely aware of possible offenses against others, especially people we work with. There are many issues that can create misunderstandings, including racial, cultural, sexual, physical, mental, and verbal issues. To be totally effective and avoid unintentional offense, you need to understand the effects of perception, cultural background, discrimination, and prejudice.

Handling Diversity in the Workplace will make you more aware of the ways we can offend others; help you recognize your blind spots; provide you with ways to avoid verbal, social, and written mistakes; help you learn how to talk about your differences and your similarities; and give you new ways to deal with and relate to people.

It deals with human issues and relationships—perception, stepping on toes, personal biases, confronting prejudice against you and others, and recognizing when to laugh instead of fight. (Too much sensitivity can be as bad as too much intolerance.) And, while this book is primarily about diversity in the workplace, the information applies to all areas of corporate and community life.

Foreword

As I have worked in the arenas of Diversity and Managing Diversity over the past 12 years, I have concluded that these topics are complex and that most of us have considerable maturing to do in these areas. I have also noted that this maturation process is a journey that requires considerable time (multiple years) and effort from most of us. Finally, I have found that no step is more important than the first one on the journey, and that the nature of that first step varies with each of us. It is for these reasons that I am encouraged by *Handling Diversity in the Workplace: Communication Is the Key.*

Handling Diversity in the Workplace can serve as an effective introduction to workforce diversity—a good first step in the maturation process—in part, because it begins at the point where many persons seeking initial clarity about diversity are in their thinking. For those readers seeking to take the first step, the book will provide insights and, most importantly, provoke reflection.

I often nodded my head in agreement as I read *Handling Diversity in the Workplace;* at other times, I responded, "Yes, but . . ." or "Not necessarily." I believe that my reactions reflect the varied nature of this subject. My hope and desire is that, upon completing this book, readers will realize that their new understanding is only the tip of the iceberg—the first step in what promises to be an ongoing process of maturation in thinking and skills. Ideally, readers will be motivated to seek other works addressing diversity, and as they do, they will discover the richness and complexity of the topic. They will recognize that they indeed are on a journey, and will appreciate even more the first step offered by Kay duPont's book.

I wish the reader much success on the maturation journey.

—Dr. R. Roosevelt Thomas
American Institute for Managing Diversity

Chapter *One*

What Diversity Really Means

Chapter Objectives

▶ Define *diversity.*

▶ Realize the importance of learning to accept and work with different types of people.

▶ Recognize the changing composition of American society.

▶ Deal more effectively with the changing demographics.

Successful organizations realize that people's differences can be their strength.

Diversity . . . Everyone seems to be talking about it. Businesses offer training on it, politicians support it, the media salutes it. But what exactly is diversity? Is it race? cultural background? personality type? The answer is yes—and much more. Some people let diversity get in the way of their relationships with other people. But successful organizations realize that people's differences can be their strength—if they combine their skills, experiences, and ideas while still valuing each other as individuals. As Abraham Lincoln said, "United we stand, divided we fall."

Take a Moment

What do you think *diversity* is? Write your own definition.

_____

_____

_____

_____

Diversity Means Differences

Differences are what diversity is all about. Although many organizations are now offering diversity training for their employees, diversity is not really a skill or something for which you can be trained. *Diversity* simply means "differences," and in this book it means "differences in people." Whether diversity becomes an asset or a liability to you and your organization depends on how you use it.

Diversity can give us a distinct advantage in the workplace—and in the world. Minorities or "the oppressed" aren't the only ones who gain from a diverse environment. Each of us benefits from the depth and vitality that diversity offers. There is very little wisdom in putting together a group of people who all have the same looks, feelings, and thought processes. If we did that, at least *half* of us would be useless.

> In this book, *diversity* means "differences in people."

A Story of Diversity

Once upon a time, there lived twin princes. Although they were twins, one prince was fair and one was dark. And their personalities were as diverse as their coloring. One prince thought more, one prince felt more. One related to the world through his logic, one through his intuition. One liked to make decisions, one liked to leave things open. One was introverted, one was extroverted. The twins weren't bothered by these differences; each drew comfort from knowing that what each was not, the other was.

As the princes grew, their subjects worried about having two heirs to one seat of power, so they tried to determine which boy was stronger and wiser so he could inherit the throne. What foolishness, the princes thought. We are neither strong nor weak, wise nor stupid. We are only *different*. We were made to rule together.

When the king died, the people of the kingdom wondered who should rule. For neither prince had turned out to be better than the other—just different. Finally, the princes decided to divide the kingdom. One chose to take the majority of the land. He said his riches lay in the wealth of the earth. The other chose to inherit the majority of the citizens. His riches, he said, lay in the hearts of his people.

After the kingdoms were divided, the people who lived in each one suffered. One kingdom had great resources but not enough workers to harvest them. The other kingdom had many hands to do the harvesting but not enough resources.

Eventually, news of the kingdoms reached an old wizard who lived far away. Saddened, but not surprised, the wizard carved two magic mirrors. When she was finished, she stood before one of the mirrors and cast a spell, saying, "The more you are like others, the more they will like you." Then she stood before the other mirror and cast a second spell, saying, "The more you give others what they need, the more they will give you what you need." She sent one mirror to each king. At first, the kings were delighted with the beautiful mirrors. But they became angry when they discovered that whenever one of them looked in his mirror, he saw his brother instead of himself. Gradually, they overcame their anger and began to watch the mirrors—and each other—more often. One brother saw his twin care for his kingdom by caring for his people. The other brother saw his twin care for his people by caring for his land. Finally, they remembered again that one of them wasn't stronger, or better, or wiser—just different.

One day, the inevitable happened—the kings stood before their mirrors at the same time. They were so surprised to look into each other's eyes that, for a moment, each froze. Then one king whispered, "The more you are like others, the more they will like you." The other replied, "The more you give others what they need, the more they will give you what you need." Then one king smiled, and one king laughed. They held out their arms and stepped into the mirrors. In the middle of a road, in the middle of the two kingdoms, one king emerged from the mirrors. The two kingdoms became one again as well, and the people were healed. And far away, an old wizard smiled.

(Story adapted from *The Two Kings*, © Diane Cory)

Diversity is challenging, yes, but it's also richer, livelier, more fun, and ultimately more profitable. If the members of your organization don't recognize that diversity is a business issue that affects your ability to compete, your company can only suffer. As new technologies make distance meaningless, our diversity puts the U.S. at the forefront of a new international order. If your organization doesn't accept and embrace diversity and teach employees how to thrive in a diverse culture, how will it fit into the global economy?

Take a Moment

Every organization reflects diversity in a variety of ways. What are some of the differences you notice in the people you work with? Does your organization do anything to help people accept and adapt to each other's differences?

_____

_____

_____

The End of the Melting Pot

Americans have traditionally thought of their society as a "melting pot" in which everyone embraced the same culture and values. That model may have worked well for previous generations, when people spent their whole lives in one place or migrated in groups, because most of the people living and working in particular areas were indeed alike. But our world is far more mobile. Developments like jet aircraft, satellite TV, and the Internet are bringing diverse groups of people closer than we'd ever dreamed possible (and probably closer than some ever wanted).

Today, American society is more like my mother's vegetable soup than a melting pot. Her soup has an overall flavor and "feeling," but I can still easily see and taste the potatoes, the carrots, the meat, the beans, and all the other vegetables.

> **Today, American society is more like vegetable soup than a melting pot.**

Members of numerous ethnic and cultural groups don't want to become part of a melted whole; they want their tastes, looks, and textures to remain unique.

Although they exist happily together in the pot and contribute to the success of the soup, they are still very different. I don't have any trouble telling the potatoes from the tomatoes.

The U.S. has 265 million individual "ingredients" in its soup, each demanding his or her own rights. Members of numerous ethnic and cultural groups don't want to become part of a melted whole; they want their tastes, looks, and textures to remain unique. Perhaps for the first time in history, people are openly expressing their identities and rejoicing in their cultures without fear of being judged. *E pluribus unum* (from many, one) is no longer a valid motto, and these changes are affecting every facet of our lives—from politics and poetry to economics and entertainment.

Unfortunately, these changes can also cause problems in our relationships. You may suddenly find yourself living and working alongside people who hold attitudes and values different from yours. You may even discover that you have biases or prejudices you never knew existed. Being around people who look, believe, or act differently from you may make you feel uncomfortable. You might even be self-conscious when people from other cultures don't act as you would—or as you think they should.

Since the predominant culture usually thinks of itself as "right," it's hard for some Americans to recognize their prejudices against others. If you are a member of a minority culture or new to the U.S., you may become angry or frustrated with that attitude. Or you may feel that nobody listens to you or that you're not being taken seriously.

Dominant cultures, however, can lose their dominant status. This is happening today to the white, male-oriented culture of the U.S. workforce. Most U.S. trade, industry, and business organizations have been dominated by white* males, both in numbers and values, since the "colonies" were formed. But white males now make up only 43 percent of the workforce. By 2005, less than 15 percent of those entering the workforce will be white males. The others will be:

White* females	32 percent
Hispanic males	16 percent
Hispanic females	12 percent
Black** males	7 percent
Black** females	9 percent
Asian and other males	5 percent
Asian and other females	5 percent

(*White = Caucasian and others with light skin not listed separately)
(**Black = African American and others with dark skin not listed separately)

Part of the reason for this decline is that, during the last decade, the Asian, African American, and Hispanic populations have been increasing in the U.S., while the Caucasian population has been declining. Nearly one out of every four Americans in the 1990 census claimed African, Asian, Hispanic, or Native American ancestry, compared to only one in five in the 1980 census. By 2050, "average" U.S. residents will trace their descent to Africa, Asia, the Hispanic areas, the Pacific Islands, Arabia—almost anywhere but white Europe.

During the last decade, the Asian, African American, and Hispanic populations have been increasing in the U.S., while the Caucasian population has been declining.

Self-Check: The Changing Face of America

Take the following quiz to see how much you really know about the changing face of America. Answers appear at the end of this chapter.

1. What percent of the U.S. population is black?
   a) 12 percent   b) 25 percent   c) 38 percent
   d) 42 percent

2. During the past ten years, the Hispanic population has increased by what percent?
   a) 20 percent   b) 38 percent   c) 41 percent
   d) 53 percent

3. What percent of newcomers into the job market are native-born white males?
   a) 14.5 percent b) 25.1 percent   c) 32.6 percent
   d) 46.9 percent

4. What percent of people in the U.S. were born between 1955 and 1965?
   a) 10 percent   b) 15 percent   c) 20 percent
   d) 25 percent

5. Approximately what percent of women between the ages of 25 and 34 are now in the workforce?
   a) 32 percent   b) 58 percent   c) 66 percent
   d) 75 percent

6. Approximately what percent of all working-age women are now in the workforce?
   a) 30 percent   b) 52 percent   c) 60 percent
   d) 75 percent

7. One out of how many black households makes more than $50,000 per year?
   a) 1 out of 52   b) 1 out of 36   c) 1 out of 17
   d) 1 out of 8

8. The best-educated, most affluent households in America are of what ancestry?
   a) Hispanic   b) Asian/Pacific Islander   c) Black
   d) White

9. To be protected under the Age Discrimination Act of 1987, you must be at least:
   a) 40 years old   b) 50 years old
   c) 60 years old   d) 70 years old

10. The median age for first marriages is now:
    a) 17   b) 21   c) 25   d) 27

11. How many interracial marriages were there in the U.S. in 1993?
    a) 2 million   b) 1 million   c) 1.2 million
    d) 3 million

12. How many people listed "Other" as their racial category in the 1990 census?
    a) 2 million   b) 7 million   c) 6.8 million
    d) 9.8 million

13. The largest majority of immigrants to the U.S. comes from what country?
    a) Mexico   b) Vietnam   c) India
    d) Philippines

14. What percent of the workforce is employed by foreign-owned companies?
    a) 1 percent   b) 2 percent   c) 3 percent
    d) 4 percent

1

Accepting These Changes Is Critical

These statistics show that the potential for cross-cultural miscommunication is great. They also reflect the change that diversity is bringing to our culture, and the challenges that change poses for each of us.

Change can be hard to accept, but it's always been a part of life in this country. In 1829, Martin Van Buren, then the governor of New York, wrote to President Andrew Jackson: "The canal system of this country is being threatened by the spread of a new form of transportation known as railroads. As you may well know, railroad carriages are pulled by engines at the enormous speed of 15 miles per hour. In addition to endangering life and limb of passengers, they roar and snort their way through the countryside. The Almighty certainly never intended that people should travel at such breakneck speed."

> **Change can be hard to accept, but it's always been a part of life in this country.**

In today's mobile world, Van Buren's concerns sound quaint, but many people are expressing the same type of fear about diversity. Some people go through life totally oblivious to the differences in people and are unwilling to change when they do notice. Why? Because it's easier to fade into the woodwork, run with the pack, keep birds of a feather together, and never have to deal with our differences. That attitude can kill a business or a career very quickly.

Many years after Martin Van Buren wrote his letter, President John F. Kennedy said, "Change is the law of life. Those who look only to the past or the present are certain to miss the future." Industry leaders have always known that adjustment to change is essential for businesses to survive and grow. The same is true of governments, countries, and individuals like you and me. Each of us has to develop our ability to deal with the changes diversity brings and the way they affect our lives. We have to resist the normal human tendency to want things to stay the same. We can't fight change or diversity, and we shouldn't fear it or feel negative about it. Change is growth, and diversity is positive. We'd be out of a job without them!

Take a Moment

Think of a time when you had to deal with change in your life. How did you handle it? Did you find the change stressful or exciting? What did you do to cope? Could any of the same strategies help you deal effectively with the changes diversity can bring to your workplace?

_____

_____

_____

_____

Four Steps to Dealing with Diversity

As the world grows smaller, functioning in a diverse work environment will be as much a part of our jobs as filing or computing. The key to dealing successfully with diversity is open, honest communication. In a diverse workplace, we should all feel free to be ourselves—while treating others with respect. We should be able to tell each other when something bothers us—without overreacting. Relationships, especially in business, grow stronger with discussion and compromise. We can all work together more effectively by following these four easy steps:

> **The key to dealing successfully with diversity is open, honest communication.**

◆ **Understand and respect individual differences.**
Keep an open mind toward others who are different from you. Remember that not everyone sees things the same way you do.

◆ **Be assertive.**
Let other people know how you want to be treated, and don't be afraid to speak up if another's actions make you uncomfortable. How will people know that you find a particular expression or behavior offensive unless you tell them? And, if someone has the courage and sensitivity to tell you how you've offended them, don't get defensive—be

thankful. The only way you can correct the situation is through honest communication. Don't say, "That's not what I meant! What's the matter with you?" Say, "I'm sorry you heard it that way. That's really not what I meant. Can I clarify and tell you what I did mean?"

◆ **Learn how others want you to treat them.**
Use the New Golden Rule (sometimes called the Platinum Rule): Treat others the way they would like to be treated. If you're confused about how to pronounce an unfamiliar name, or whether a person would rather be called black or African American, ASK. Your question will not only help you learn how to avoid misunderstandings and conflict but also will communicate a respect that will strengthen your relationships.

◆ **Act as a force for change.**
Everyone is responsible for workplace behavior. If you encounter an example of discrimination or prejudice, speak up. Tell the people involved why you think the behavior was inappropriate. You may not be able to change attitudes overnight, but you can change behavior, and that's the first step.

We will explore these steps further throughout the rest of this book. In the next chapter, we will discuss some of the factors that make up our individual differences. In Chapter 3, we will consider the attitudes and behaviors that keep us from being able to accept and respect those differences. Chapter 4 offers strategies for communicating effectively with people from a variety of cultures and backgrounds, and Chapter 5 presents ways you can make your own communication needs and preferences known. We will conclude with suggestions for ways you can continue to act as a force for change in developing and maintaining a diverse workplace.

Everyone is responsible for workplace behavior.

1

As Ralph Waldo Emerson observed, fear springs from ignorance. Understanding more about how people are similar and different will help us overcome our fear of diversity and learn to see our differences as strengths instead of weaknesses.

Quote

We have an American problem. It can only be solved by all Americans working together . . . . I want you to find strength in your diversity. Let the fact that you are black or yellow or white be a source of pride and inspiration to you. Draw strength from it. Let it be someone else's problem, but never yours. Never hide behind it or use it as an excuse for not doing your best. We all have to live here together . . . . Divided, fighting among ourselves, walking our separate lines of diversity, we are as weak as newborn babies.

Gen. Colin Powell
Former Chair, U.S. Joint Chiefs of Staff

Self-Check: Chapter 1 Review

Answers appear on page 103.

1. We can define *diversity* as:

    _____

2. By the year 2005, what percent of people entering the workforce will be white males?

    _____

3. Successful organizations realize that people's differences can be their _____

4. Today, the U.S. is much more like _____ than a melting pot.

5. True or False?
    By the year 2050, the "average" U.S. resident will be a Caucasian of European ancestry.

The Changing Face of America
Quiz Answers

1. *What percent of the U.S. population is black?*
   Answer: a) 12 percent. More than 25 percent of Americans are people of color (blacks, Asians, Pacific Islanders, and Hispanics). Eleven percent of management/professional people are black.

2. *During the past ten years, the Hispanic population has increased by what percent?*
   Answer: d) 53 percent. Hispanics are the fastest-growing minority in the U.S. (Caucasians have increased only 35 percent in the last ten years.) Hispanics now number about 24 million and are expected to increase another 48 percent by 1999. By the year 2010, Hispanics will be the largest minority in America.

3. *What percent of newcomers into the job market are native-born white males?*
   Answer: a) 14.5 percent. The late 1980s saw this figure go below 50 percent for the first time in history, and it has continued to drop. (It is important to remember that these predictions refer to growth. This means that while males will still have dominance, with an expected 38 percent of the total workforce in 2005, they will be decreasing in numbers of new hires.)

4. *What percent of people in the U.S. were born between 1955 and 1965?*
   Answer: d) 25 percent. There are 49 million of these 30- to 40-year-olds (baby boomers), and they are changing the economic and social structure of America.

5. *Approximately what percent of women between the ages of 25 and 34 are now in the workforce?*
   Answer: d) 75 percent. Because these are the childbearing years, this will affect the way companies treat child care and maternity/paternity leave.

6. *Approximately what percent of all working-age women are now in the workforce?*
   Answer: c) 60 percent. Less than 75 percent of all working-age men are in the workforce. Women in management have increased 24 percent since 1980; they now number 6.1 million. John Naisbitt, author of *Megatrends,* believes the changing role of women in our society is the most significant change in this century.

7. *One out of how many black households makes more than $50,000 per year?*
   Answer: d) 1 out of 8 (13 percent).

8. *The best-educated, most affluent households in America are of what ancestry?*
   Answer: b) Asian/Pacific Islander. Asians have the highest income per household (not per individual, however), with more than 32 percent earning more than $50,000 per year, contrasted with 29 percent of Caucasian families. They also have the highest number of people with more than five years of college. And 39 percent of Asian Americans finish college, compared to 17 percent for the general population.

9. *To be protected under the Age Discrimination Act of 1987, you must be at least:*
   Answer: a) 40 years old.

10. *The median age for first marriages is now:*
    Answer: c) 25 (up three years since 1975).

11. *How many interracial marriages were there in the U.S. in 1993?*
    Answer: c) 1.2 million, as contrasted with only 200,000 in 1960. Interracial and interethnic marriage is not new. But during the past two decades, America has produced the greatest variety of hybrid households in the history of the world. As ever-increasing numbers of couples break through racial, ethnic, and religious barriers to invent a life together, we must rethink and redefine our views about these unions.

1

12. *How many people listed "Other" as their racial category in the 1990 census?*
   Answer: d) 9.8 million (4 percent), as contrasted with 200,000 in 1960.

13. *The largest majority of immigrants to the U.S. comes from what country?*
   Answer: a) Mexico (6.2 million). The Philippines ranks second, with 1 million.

14. *What percent of the workforce is employed by foreign-owned companies?*
   Answer: d) 4 percent.

Quote

What we need in the United States is not division. What we need in the United States is not hatred. What we need in the United States is not violence or lawlessness, but love and wisdom and compassion toward one another. And a feeling of justice toward those who still suffer within our country, whether they be white or they be black. Let us dedicate ourselves to what the Greeks wrote so many years ago: To tame the savageness of man and make gentle the life of this world, let us dedicate ourselves to that and say a prayer for our country and our people.

Robert F. Kennedy
Former U.S. Attorney General and U.S. Senator

Chapter *Two*

Factors That Create Diversity

Chapter Objectives

► Identify the factors of diversity.

► Recognize different personality styles and adjust to them.

► Adjust your assertiveness level to match someone else's.

► Deal more effectively with the opposite gender.

> **Diversity is much more than skin color, gender, or background.**

Diversity is much more than skin color, gender, or background. It's internal and external. Skin color is the result of the level of pigment in our skin; it's a biological event. It doesn't determine how we think, feel, or believe. Gender is random gene selection; we had no choice. It doesn't decide our goals, ambitions, or careers. As children, we learn about morals, values, and religious beliefs. But these may be relearned, changed, and adjusted over the course of our lives. Each of us is diverse in many ways—chosen and random—and each of us brings many qualities to the workforce and the world in general.

I, for instance, am extremely diverse: I am female (still a minority in this country). I am under 5 feet tall, so the government officially lists me as a midget (that's certainly a minority). My father is a Catholic from the North, and my mother is a Baptist from the South. I am Jewish. My grandparents were French, English, Irish, and Native American. I am American by birth and Southern by choice, but I've traveled extensively and worked in many other countries. And now, my doctor says I am "chronologically gifted" and "poundage enhanced"! Am I different from you in a lot of ways? What other factors could I have listed?

Take a Moment

List as many factors as you can that go into diversity—all
the things that make us different as human beings:

_____

_____

_____

What types of diversity are present in you? in someone you
work closely with?

_____

_____

_____

2

What Makes Us Diverse?

When we put all people of one color, gender, or ethnic group
into one category, we disregard the many other ways in which
people are diverse. Many of the factors that create diversity may
not be immediately visible: personality style, thinking style,
processing style, assertiveness level, religion, values, energy level,
habits, likes and dislikes, education and knowledge, goals and
ambitions, political views, lifestyle, sexual orientation, social
status, job titles, and many others. We can find diversity even in
a group of 25-year-old, native-born, white males of the same
religion, size, and coloring. *Diversity* simply means "differences,"
and no two people are identical.

**Many of the
factors that
create diversity
may not be
immediately
visible.**

25

Some of the ways people are diverse include:

◆ Processing Style

◆ Assertiveness Level

◆ Age

◆ Gender

◆ Race

◆ Disability

Processing Style as a Factor in Diversity

Processing
style **is the way**
people listen,
receive, think
about, and
accept
information.

Processing style is the way people listen, receive, think about, and accept information. It is subconscious and automatic, although it might change because of age or disability. We can identify three major categories of processing styles:

◆ Seers (visual)

◆ Hearers (auditory)

◆ Feelers (kinesthetic)

"Seers" prefer to receive information visually. They like to read, and they want information given to them in written form. If you call a highly visual person on the phone and say, "Here is what I need you to do," he or she might say, "Would you send me a fax on that?" No matter how many times you *tell* them, they need to see it.

"Hearers" will ask for information in an auditory form, usually the phone. If you send them a note, they will say, "Yes, I saw it, but I didn't have time to work on it. Can we talk about it now?" No matter how many e-mails you send them, they'll still want to *hear* it.

"Feelers" want to meet about the matter. They like to see your face, be able to *feel* your presence. If you write or call, they'll still want to get together.

How do you figure out which style you're dealing with? All you have to do is watch and listen—most people broadcast their styles (particularly when they are *against* an idea). Seers use visual words. "I can't *visualize* how that would work." "I need the *big picture* here." They can be listening to a radio and say, "Did you see what he said?" They may also be reading or writing when you see them. They have notes in their pockets and purses. They enjoy reading, watching TV, and playing intellectual games.

Hearers use auditory words: "I like the way that *sounds.*" "Are we *in tune* on this issue?" If they're not listening to music or tapes, they may be whistling or humming. Sometimes they might not even realize they are doing it. They enjoy word games, conversation, and movies.

Feelers use feeling words: "This is a *touchy* issue." "This doesn't *feel* right." They also like the sensory perception of touching things and people. They like to hold items while they talk. And, if they compliment your clothing, they may reach out and touch it at the same time. They will also wear soft, sometimes fuzzy, materials. They enjoy sports, concerts and plays, and dancing.

If you need additional proof of a coworker's processing style, ask a leading question: "How does this idea *look* to you?" If the person is a seer, he or she will say "Fine" or "It looks great." If your coworker answers in a mode you didn't use ("*Sounds* good to me"), try a question in that mode: "I'm glad you like it. I have another angle I'd like you to *listen to.* How does this *sound?*" If you get another response in the same mode, you've probably found that person's favorite style. Try communicating with that person in that style as much as possible.

Of course, people cross over from one style to another, but researchers say that we stay in our own comfort style 70 percent of the time. So identifying and adapting to someone's primary style can be an effective way of communicating with them. Remember: The more you are like others, the more they will like you.

2

Seers use visual words, hearers use auditory words, and feelers use feeling words.

We stay in our own comfort style 70 percent of the time.

Take a Moment

Ask a friend or coworker to describe something—a vacation, a picture, a person. Listen to the type of language they use. Do you hear visual words, auditory words, or feeling words?

Assertiveness Level as a Factor in Diversity

Assertiveness is another factor that can influence diversity. *Assertiveness* can be defined as the power we use to make our needs, wants, and desires known to others. (*Assertiveness* should not be confused with *aggressiveness,* which involves trying to dominate other people.)

> *Assertiveness can be defined as the power we use to make our needs, wants, and desires known to others.*

People express assertiveness in many different ways: through tone and volume of voice, gestures, physical size and posture, and by what they say. As you might guess, different people express different levels of assertiveness. A person who speaks in a high, soft voice while looking at the ground would be perceived as less assertive than a person who stands straight, looks a person in the eye, and speaks loudly.

We can represent these differences in assertiveness on a scale. Those who express less power vocally and physically would be on the lower on the end of the scale. People on the high end of the scale seem to have more power—conveying their needs, wants, and desires more effectively and getting more results.

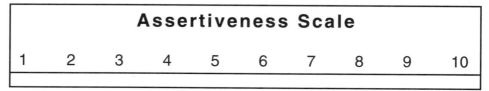

Assertiveness Scale

1	2	3	4	5	6	7	8	9	10

As with other types of diversity, these variations in assertiveness can cause problems if we aren't aware of them. The farther apart two people are on the assertiveness scale, the more potential there is for misunderstanding and conflict. A person who rates a 10 on the scale may have very little respect for a person who rates a 2, and vice versa. (Many cultures have a much lower assertiveness level than Americans. They may see our brashness as a sign of disrespect and egotistical behavior, while Americans may see a lack of assertion as passivity or weakness.)

You can't change another person's level of assertiveness, but you can deal effectively with people of different assertiveness levels by adjusting your level to meet theirs. Try to determine how assertive the other person is and adjust your behavior accordingly. When speaking with people on the lower end of the scale, try lowering the volume of your voice and pausing occasionally to give them a chance to talk. When speaking with highly assertive people, increase the volume of your voice, and don't be afraid to express your opinion. Just remember, you can't change *them;* you have to change *yourself.*

2

Take a Moment

Where do you think you rank on the assertiveness scale in your normal dealings at work? Where does the coworker with whom you work most closely rank? Where does your manager rank? How can you adjust your assertiveness level to match theirs?

Personality Type as a Factor in Diversity

Some people love to work in teams; some are loners. Some people want facts and figures before they make a decision; some go with a gut feeling. Some people are cheerful all the time; others seem to have the weight of the world on their shoulders. Throughout history, people have tried to explain differences in personality. Astrology was one early attempt that identified 12 different personality types, or signs; there have been many others.

In 1923, Dr. Carl Jung created a model based on four categories of personality types: Intuitor, Thinker, Feeler, and Sensor. Since then, many researchers have expanded on Jung's model. Today, dozens of models of personality types exist, all based on grouping behavior into four categories. Though the names used to describe the different personality types differ in each model, the personality types themselves remain the same.[1]

---

[1] If you are interested in more information on personality types, see the AMI video *Relationship Strategies* with Dr. Tony Alessandra.

● Factors That Create Diversity

I like to use dogs to represent different behavioral styles. Read through the following descriptions, and see if you can identify yourself and your coworkers:

Bulldog

- Task-oriented
- Motivated by achievement
- Fears being taken advantage of
- Favorite words: *time, more, money, deal, power*
- Annoyed by people who waste his/her time
- Takes risks, accepts challenges
- Focuses on the bottom line
- Speaks first, thinks later
- Gets the job done—quickly
- Sees the big picture easily
- Expresses opinions freely
- Appears rushed, insensitive
- Not concerned with details
- Challenges others frequently
- Doesn't listen completely or with empathy
- Impatient, confronting, controlling
- Sometimes perceived as rude, overbearing
- Extrovert
- Aggressive

Retriever

- Task-oriented
- Highly analytical
- Motivated by order
- Fears losing control of own situation
- Favorite words: *logic, sense, proof*
- Annoyed by emotion, rambling
- Believes his/her way is only way
- Controlled, critical, cautious
- Concentrates on details
- Works best under known conditions
- Focuses on one thing at a time
- Checks for accuracy
- Thinks logically
- Talks very little
- Critiques performance (own and others')
- Makes slow but excellent decisions
- Sometimes perceived as unemotional
- Introvert
- Passive until challenged

Spaniel

- People-oriented
- Motivated by recognition
- Fears not being liked
- Favorite words: *I, me*
- Annoyed by people who interrupt and those who don't recognize his/her talents
- Makes decisions emotionally
- Likes to be in contact with people
- Makes favorable impression
- Verbalizes, articulates well
- Talks a lot
- Influencing, interacting, interesting
- Generates enthusiasm
- Likes to be fashionable
- Entertaining
- Wants to help
- Participates in groups
- Sometimes perceived as flighty
- Extrovert
- Assertive

Collie

- People-oriented
- Fears change
- Patient, steady
- Favorite words: *we, us, others, team*
- Annoyed by people who disturb his/her belongings and those who don't keep their promises
- Motivated by stability and teamwork
- Makes decisions slowly
- Performs accepted work pattern
- Can remain in one place for long periods
- Loyal and supportive
- Specializes in one or two areas
- Team builder
- Concentrates on one thing at a time
- Shows loyalty and support
- Listens well
- Calms excited people
- Sometimes perceived as stubborn and slow
- Introvert
- Passive

© Kay duPont

We all have parts of each personality type, of course, but tend to stay in one or two styles most of the time. The ideal team would consist of equal numbers of each personality: Bulldogs to generate ideas and insist on results, Spaniels to go out and promote those ideas, Collies to make sure the ideas are carried out and bring stability to the group, and Retrievers to make certain that key details are covered and the project is done well.

Unfortunately, instead of capitalizing on our differences to work more effectively, we let them come between us. Can you see the potential for conflict in the following interaction between Sally Bulldog and Jeff Collie?

Sally:
You're spending too much time talking to customers. You're supposed to be stocking shelves, not visiting.

Jeff:
I'm just trying to keep the customers happy. Some of them have questions or just want to talk.

Sally:
You're not being paid to talk. Stop being so nice and get to work.

Sally doesn't realize it, but her task-oriented Bulldog approach has alienated people-oriented Jeff. In fact, Sally may have destroyed their relationship. As a Bulldog, Sally has no idea what she's done. And, because Collies dislike conflict, Jeff probably won't tell her.

As this example illustrates, most people don't carry a crystal ball in their pocket. The key to dealing with the different personality types is to develop all four sides of our own personalities so we can adjust ourselves to the people we meet. If Sally developed the Collie side of her personality, she'd deal more sensitively with Jeff. If Jeff developed the Bulldog side of his personality, he'd be more comfortable explaining himself to Sally when a communication problem arose.

2

The ideal team would consist of equal numbers of each personality.

Unfortunately, instead of capitalizing on our differences to work more effectively, we let them come between us.

Here are some specific guidelines for getting along with the four personality types:

Bulldogs:
- Get to the point and stick to the facts.
- Compliment their ideas and goals, not them personally.
- Motivate them with clear objectives; they won't listen to vague directions.
- Give them several options, and let them choose.
- Assure them that their time will not be wasted.
- Give them more than what they expected, and make sure they know you did it.
- Don't expect recognition; they don't have enough time to give praise.
- Respect their authority.
- Never be late.
- Give them 110%.

Retrievers:
- Be organized and armed with facts and statistics.
- Compliment their efficiency.
- Communicate systematically.
- Motivate logically.
- Don't rush their decision-making process.
- Avoid emotion.
- Check your timing—they can only do one thing at a time.
- Don't take their attitude personally.
- Avoid small talk and personal questions.
- Don't expect compliments or gifts.
- Remind them of events and things to be done outside their field of concentration.
- Let them think the plan was their idea.

Spaniels:
- Be entertaining.
- Pay them direct compliments.
- Allow them plenty of time to state their case.
- Support their dreams and opinions.
- Summarize in writing what you both agreed to; they get so caught up being the center of attention that they sometimes forget.
- Offer incentives and testimonials as motivation.
- Listen for facts and feelings.
- Probe them with direct questions.
- Establish checkpoints or follow-up procedures.
- Let them be the center of attention.

Collies:
- Show them personal interest before getting to the subject.
- Discuss their feelings along with the facts.
- Compliment their efforts, credibility, and loyalty.
- Motivate them by helping them strengthen their relationships.
- Give them a mentor.
- Actively listen and discuss alternatives slowly. (They are not dense, but it takes them time to think things through.)
- Offer personal assurances that you will stand by their decisions.
- Don't push them or make them feel like they are getting the third degree.

Take a Moment

Can you identify your dominant and secondary personality styles? How would developing the other styles in your personality help you in your work?

2

Age as a Factor in Diversity

America is getting older. A Census Bureau study predicts that the 65-and-older population will grow from 1 in 8 today to 1 in 6 by 2020. At that time, America's elderly population will total 53.3 million—a 63 percent increase over the current total.

> **Age creates a diversity issue because younger workers want different rewards than older ones.**

The median age of workers will rise from 37 in 1990 to 41 in 2005. Workers over the age of 45 are expected to total close to 58 million by 2005, and because of improved health, many of these workers will be over today's "retirement" age.

Age creates a diversity issue because younger workers want different rewards than older ones. Older people are more likely to be motivated by appeals to intuition, feelings, and the complex nature of reality rather than appeals to intellect, reason, and power. They are used to working in hierarchical organizations and are willing to work hard to make good money.

Younger people don't work for *money;* they work for *rewards.* They have a different idea of what's important and a different work ethic. Today's young people want to be part of a business *team,* not a hierarchical bureaucracy. They don't want to be told what to do; they want to be empowered.

The more an organization operates in the traditional pyramid style, the less younger workers are going to like it. Unfortunately, the more organizations adopt self-managing teams, the less older workers will like it, because they aren't used to that style of management. To adapt to these very different work styles, organizations that employ both older and younger workers need to develop a management style that provides some structure, while still allowing for the personal growth of employees.

Gender as a Factor in Diversity

In today's business world, men and women work side by side in careers of all kinds. For the most part, there are no more "female" jobs or "male" roles in business. Consequently, men and women are asked every day to relate to each other in new (and equal) ways, and that makes some people uncomfortable. Most of us began our journey to adulthood in same-sex groups: the girls sat on one side of the room, the boys sat on the other.

In our culture, females are traditionally taught to be nonaggressive, noncompetitive, submissive, and dependent; they learn to put relationships ahead of winning. Males, on the other hand, learn how to compete early in life; they are expected to be aggressive, dominant, independent, and competitive. A Harvard study shows that American mothers are generally more verbal with daughters than with sons, teaching their girls how to nurture and build relationships. Other studies show that parents handle male infants more roughly than female infants and speak to them in louder voices, teaching their boys how to be tough. Parents may instill differences in many other subtle ways, but the result is the same: starkly different communication and working styles.

> **When men succeed, they are likely to praise their own abilities; women credit their success to luck, extra effort, or the contributions of others.**

Men and women are also brought up to have different beliefs about succeeding or failing at a task. When men succeed, they are likely to praise their own abilities; women credit their success to luck, extra effort, or the contributions of others. When men fail, they are likely to blame someone or something else; women tend to take failure personally.

Given these differences in upbringing, it's surprising that men and women can communicate with each other at all. Because we tend to expect others to respond as we do and often consider differences to be "wrong," communication between the sexes holds many opportunities for wrong assumptions, frustration, and hurt feelings. But to interact effectively in our diverse workplace, we need to accept each individual as a *person,* not a *male* or a *female.*

Self-Check: Gender Differences

Take the following quiz to see how much you really know about how the genders communicate. Answers appear at the end of this chapter.

Indicate **True** or **False** for each statement.

_____ 1. Women talk more than men.

_____ 2. Women interrupt men more frequently than men interrupt women.

_____ 3. Men look at women more often when conversing with them than women look at men.

_____ 4. Women talk about a wider range of subjects than men.

_____ 5. In conversation, a woman generally nods to show that she agrees with the speaker.

_____ 6. Women speak more politely than men.

_____ 7. Men and women use the same set of words.

_____ 8. Men are harder on themselves and blame themselves more.

_____ 9. Women ask more questions.

_____10. Women are more intuitive than men.

_____11. At business meetings, people are more likely to listen to men than women.

_____12. Men and women laugh at the same things.

_____13. Women touch others more often.

_____14. Women confront problems more directly and are likely to bring up a problem first.

So, career equality notwithstanding, men and women are different. We listen differently, talk differently, and build relationships differently. According to couples' therapist John Gray, in *Men Are from Mars, Women Are from Venus,* men and women also "think, feel, perceive, react, respond, love, need, and appreciate each other differently." The biggest difference is that men's genetic makeup prepares them to be strong protectors, while women excel as peacemakers. Men are hunters by nature and usually prefer to work side by side with other men, with little verbal interaction. Women are nurturers by nature and usually prefer to make face-to-face contact, talking more frequently and more intensely. Men favor information over emotion. They use "report talk" and focus on their independence and status. Women favor emotion over information and use "rapport talk." They strive to maintain intimacy and create connections. These differences cause us to see each other as opposites, not complements.

> To communicate better and coexist more easily, men and women need to acknowledge their differences and appreciate where each excels.

To communicate better and coexist more easily, men and women need to acknowledge their differences and appreciate where each excels. They should also adopt some of the communication techniques of the opposite gender. Suzette Elgin says in *The Last Word on the Gentle Art of Verbal Self-Defense* that in every conversation, you must make adjustments based on the listener's reaction to what you've said. There are few communication strategies that will fail more quickly than being determined to talk in a particular way—your way—no matter what else happens. This is especially true when talking with the opposite gender. For women speaking to men, the most effective adaptation is to move from a *feeling* style to a *content* style. Women need to make a conscious effort to:

> For women speaking to men, the most effective adaptation is to move from a *feeling* style to a *content* style.

◆ Get to the point quicker; avoid rambling and using filler phrases.

◆ Use more "earthy" humor—humor that is related to topics other than children and themselves.

◆ Learn about (or at least read about) sports, and bring up the topic first in conversation.

◆ In mixed groups, talk about things other than people and surroundings.

◆ Answer questions more directly.

◆ Be more authoritative and take more control.

◆ Be honest when you're angry.

◆ Don't be afraid of confrontation.

◆ Compliment men on their achievements, not on them as individuals.

◆ Avoid tag endings and confirming questions at the end of statements ("I have been in this position for, what? Three years? Isn't that right?").

◆ *Be patient.*

Men can converse with women more effectively by moving from a totally factual style to a more emotional level. Men need to make a conscious effort to:

◆ Listen more closely (or at least exhibit listening behavior).

◆ Paraphrase and clarify (without parroting) what the woman is saying.

◆ Talk about feelings—if not yours, then at least hers.

◆ Talk about people, not just things.

◆ Ask about intent, not just content.

◆ Avoid nicknames for women (such as "gals," "ladies," and "Hon").

◆ Compliment women on themselves, not just on their achievements.

◆ Talk about things other than sports and business in mixed groups.

◆ Ask more, tell less.

◆ Avoid discounting or "one-upping" others' ideas.

◆ *Be patient.*

Men can converse with women more effectively by moving from a totally factual style to a more emotional level.

2

Men will never be like women, and women will never be like men. We have different ways of communicating, listening, moving, thinking, and even sleeping. And, just between you and me, isn't that the way we prefer it?

Just remember that habits can be broken. Just because Mama or Daddy communicated in a particular fashion doesn't mean you have to. Both sexes need to cultivate strong, useful communication styles and rid themselves of communication habits that are not serving them well. By learning to recognize, appreciate, and adjust for our differences—and our similarities—men and women in all types of personal and business relationships can avoid the problems that result from miscommunication.

> **Both sexes need to cultivate strong, useful communication styles and rid themselves of communication habits that are not serving them well.**

Race as a Factor in Diversity

People of color (African Americans, others who are considered black, Hispanics, Asians, Pacific Islanders) currently make up a little more than one quarter of the U.S. population. Due to higher immigration and birth rates, these minority groups are growing at a faster rate than the U.S. Caucasian population. By the year 2030, people of color will make up approximately 43 percent of the nation's population and will claim 50 percent by the middle of the next century.

Blacks currently make up 13 percent of the total U.S. population. In 1993, blacks represented 11 percent of total occupational employment and held 7 percent of all professional and managerial jobs.

> **Due to higher immigration and birth rates, minority groups are growing at a faster rate than the U.S. Caucasian population.**

The number of Hispanics in America has doubled in the last ten years; they now make up 10 percent of the total population. Asians and Pacific Islanders are this country's fastest-growing minority group. In the last ten years, their numbers have increased by almost 80 percent, and they now make up 4 percent of the total population.

Even with this large increase in minority cultures, many Americans are still reluctant to teach their children about ethnic diversity. When asked to describe their earliest race-related memories and the feelings associated with them, both white children and children of color often report feelings of confusion, anxiety, and fear. Consider, for example, the small white child in the mall with his mother who asks, "Why is that kid black?" The embarrassed mother replies, "Shhh. Don't say that." The child was only attempting to make sense of a new observation, yet the mother's attempt to silence him sends a message that it is not okay to talk about this observation (and possibly even skin color). Caucasian children quickly become aware that their questions about race raise adult anxiety, and as a result, they learn not to ask.

People of color often have early memories of name-calling or other negative interactions with other children, and sometimes with adults. They also report having had questions that went both unasked and unanswered. Forty-five percent of U.S. students in grades 6 through 12 say that they have experienced prejudice from their peers in the past year. (Asians have the highest rate of experienced prejudice.) In addition, many people have had uncomfortable interchanges around race-related topics as adults.

We must learn to treat people equally and objectively. We must recognize people's differences but not allow ourselves—or others—to condemn, belittle, or discriminate because of them. We are all minorities—everyone in America, including Native Americans, came from somewhere else. The sooner we can learn to live together, the better our business and social relationships will be.

We must learn to treat people equally and objectively.

Whites must stop thinking of themselves as the superior race or the "right" color or even the "majority." Blacks must realize that the people they work with today are not the same people who enslaved their ancestors generations ago. Hispanics must forgive whites for the intolerable acts perpetrated at the Alamo. Native Americans must not blame their present coworkers for the way their ancestors were treated by European settlers. None of us should be criticized, ostracized, or demoralized for history. In order to work together, we must concentrate on our strengths and respect each other as individuals and as members of unique and different cultures. We do not have to be clones to be equals.

Quote

Race is an arbitrary and meaningless concept. Races among humans don't exist. If there ever was any such thing as race, there has been so much constant crisscrossing of genes for the last 500,000 years that it would have lost all meaning anyway. There are no real divisions between us, only a continuum of variations that constantly change, as we come together and separate according to the movement of human populations.

Amoja Three Rivers
Cultural Etiquette: A Guide for the Well-Intentioned

Disability as a Factor in Diversity

There are 43 million people with disabilities in the United States, and they're not hiding anymore. As physically challenged people are mainstreamed into society, they become handicapped—not by their different abilities but by the attitudes toward them. Although the disabled have as many valid ideas and leadership abilities as the nondisabled, many able-bodied people are unable to look beyond the disability. To change existing attitudes toward those with disabilities, we need to improve communication between all involved. It takes more than a warm heart to break down barriers.

> As physically challenged people are mainstreamed into society, they become handicapped— not by their different abilities but by the attitudes toward them.

Disabilities are often physical and visible, but there are many hidden disabilities, like arthritis, hearing or visual impairment, cancer, or loss of a breast or some other unseen body part. There are also personal disabilities like height, weight, and thinning hair. Oddly, people often react negatively to visible disabilities, such as loss of limbs, blindness, obesity, or severe height differences, but they react sympathetically when they learn of invisible impairments.

Organizations are sometimes afraid to hire a differently abled person, often because they fear that it would be too hard to let that person go if the person didn't work out. This concern can be overcome simply by realizing that physically challenged people are mentally as capable as anyone else. Blind people can often function more aptly with their hands, hear better, and work a computer better than people with full sight. A person in a wheelchair may drive a hand-controlled car much more skillfully than an able-bodied person can drive a regular car, and certainly being in a chair will not affect their computer or office skills. A person who is trained to work a computer by voice is no less capable than someone who is trained to operate a computer by hand. People with disabilities are only restricted in a specific area, and in the long run, may not be handicapped at all. Take the time to discover the true depth of a person's independence and avoid making assumptions.

If you work with someone who is differently abled, learn to talk about it. You don't have to avoid the subject; a person in a wheelchair *knows* that he or she is in the chair! But do be aware and sensitive. I called for a volunteer to come onstage recently, and a blind woman jumped to her feet. Her dog jumped to his feet at the same time, and they came bounding up the stage steps. I spoke to the woman and to her dog, and then we proceeded with the demonstration. When we were finished, I told her I would send her a copy of one of my books as a reward for coming onstage. As I thought about this later, I *realized* that she was blind. I *knew* she was blind when she volunteered, but she was so lively and eager and full of fun that the *realization* didn't sink in until later. I could have sent the book, but because I try to be aware and sensitive, I called her and asked whether she would like a book or an audiotape. She was thrilled that I noticed our differences and wanted her to have the right gift for *her*. If you work with someone who is visually impaired, *ask* them if they would like help. If you work with someone who stutters, *ask* them if they would like you to help with a difficult word now and then. (Most stutterers become annoyed with people who continually finish sentences for them.)

If someone has no visible problem, but has a certain habit, be sensitive enough to ask for a deeper explanation. A person who asks you to repeat your statements may be hearing impaired; a person who becomes short-winded may have heart problems; a person who is overweight may have a thyroid deficiency. Making fun of someone because they can't keep up with you in every way is a form of bigotry.

> **If you work with someone who is differently abled, learn to talk about it.**

If you're the person with the disability, understand that most people will be curious in the beginning—acknowledge that rather than being defensive.

If you're the person with the disability, understand that most people will be curious in the beginning—acknowledge that rather than being defensive. In the Tennessee Williams play *The Glass Menagerie,* the young Laura let her entire life be ruined because she had to wear a leg brace in school. She believed that no one would like her because of it. Many years later, she learned that no one could hear her brace hitting the stairs and that the boy she cared about in high school thought she was beautiful. Each of us has a disability of some sort—no one is perfect! Letting our hidden or visible differences make our life miserable, or blaming our differences for our misfortunes, is not a good idea. Learn to be outgoing, honest, and friendly. Few handicaps are so bad that others will not overlook them if you do.

Putting the Factors Together

There is more to diversity than meets the eye. People are made up of personality style, processing style, assertiveness level, religion, values, energy level, habits, likes and dislikes, education and knowledge, goals and ambitions, political views, lifestyle, sexual orientation, social status, job titles, and many other things. No two people are identical, and even if one of us is right, the other does not have to be wrong. We must learn to accept people for who they are, not who we want them to be.

Quote

Where, after all, do universal human rights begin? In small places, close to home. So close and so small that they cannot be seen on any maps of the world. Yet they are the world of the individual persons; the neighborhood they live in; the school or college they attend; the factory, farm, or office where they work. Such are the places where every man, woman, and child seeks equal justice, equal opportunity, equal dignity without discrimination. Unless these rights have meaning there, they have little meaning anywhere.

Eleanor Roosevelt
Former First Lady and
U.S. Delegate to the United Nations

Self-Check: Chapter 2 Review

Answers appear on page 103.

1. True or False?
   Diversity is mostly an issue of skin color and gender.

2. The three major categories of processing styles are:

   _____

   _____

   _____

3. True or False?
   To work most effectively with other people, you should identify their assertiveness level and adjust your own to match.

4. Match the following personality types with their characteristics:
   _____ Bulldog
   _____ Retriever
   _____ Spaniel
   _____ Collie

   a. Task-oriented, motivated by order, concentrates on details
   b. People-oriented, motivated by stability and teamwork, loyal and supportive
   c. People-oriented, motivated by recognition, generates enthusiasm
   d. Task-oriented, motivated by achievement, focused on the bottom line

5. Young people don't work for _____;
   they work for _____.

6. True or False?
   Thanks to changing attitudes, men and women now behave in virtually the same way.

7. True or False?
   People of color make up more than one-fourth of the U.S. population.

43

Gender Quiz Answers

1. *Women talk more than men.*
    False: Contrary to popular stereotypes, men actually talk more. They also talk for longer periods of time and more often than women in a mixed group. Studies like one done by linguist Ned Hershman show that men give answers that are lengthier and more involved than the questions asked. One study found that women spoke an average of three minutes when asked to describe a painting, and men averaged 13 minutes. Because of this, women often withdraw from conversations and speak less than men in mixed conversations.

2. *Women interrupt men more frequently than men interrupt women.*
    False: University of California researchers Donald Zimmerman and Candice West found that 75–98 percent of all interruptions are made by men. They also found that, after being interrupted by men, women become increasingly quiet, pausing more than normal after speaking. Men are also more likely to answer questions that are not even posed to them. And they are more likely to openly challenge and dispute what someone else says. In single-sex groups, though, men and women interrupt each other equally.

3. *Men look at women more often when conversing with them than women look at men.*
    False: Numerous studies show that women make better eye contact and focus on a speaker, male or female, more steadily than men. For that reason, women appear to be more attentive when listening. A study by Dr. Albert Mehrabian, reported in his book *Silent Messages,* shows that in positive interactions, women increase their eye contact. Men tend to be uncomfortable in their interactions and decrease their eye contact (except in conflict). Women also appear friendlier than men when meeting and greeting people. Women smile 93 percent of the time, men only 57 percent of the time.

4. *Women talk about a wider range of subjects than men.*
    True: A study by Pam Fischman of Queens College in New York verified that over 60 percent of the topics introduced into conversations are introduced by women. Women

generally want to talk problems out, and they use
conversation to gain a sympathetic ear or understanding.
Men use conversation for defining problems and finding
solutions. Even though men don't bring up as many topics of
conversation as women, they interrupt more, which actually
gives them control of the topics.

5. *In conversation, a woman generally nods to show that she agrees
with the speaker.*
False: Studies consistently show that women show approval
by smiling. They nod to acknowledge the speaker and
indicate that they are listening. Men nod when they *agree*
with the speaker. As a result, men often presume that women
are agreeing when they aren't, and women see men as
uninterested or not listening. Sally McDonald Ginnett's
research at Cornell University found that women are also
more inclined to say "uh-huh" to encourage the speaker
when listening. When men make listening responses, it's
usually because they *disagree* with what the person is saying.
As a result, men perceive women as uncritical listeners or
even as flirting; women see men as arrogant.

6. *Women speak more politely than men.*
True: Women use more filler words, as well as "women only"
constructions ("It's really just so wonderful to see how nice
everyone looks; I hope you wouldn't really mind if . . ."). As
a result, men don't get the true message, or they don't take
women seriously. According to Mary Richie Key, an expert
on women's speech, women tend to be more tentative when
they speak because they generally communicate from a
weaker position. In her book *Language in a Woman's Place,*
Robin Laycoff says women's use of "tag endings," such as
asking a question after making a statement ("It's a lovely
party, isn't it?"), adds to the image of being unsure of
themselves. Women are also less likely to use command
terms. They will say, "Would you mind getting me a cup of
coffee?" instead of a man's more direct, "Get me a cup of
coffee."

7. *Men and women use the same set of words.*
   False: Women talk about feelings, relationships, people, children, and self-improvement. Men talk about news, sports, money, business, and physical tasks. Men also tend to bring up fewer personal topics than women.

8. *Men are harder on themselves and blame themselves more.*
   False: Women tend to be more self-critical. They may personalize a problem, take responsibility for it, or blame themselves when they may have had no part in it at all.

9. *Women ask more questions.*
   True: Just as women bring up more topics in conversation, they also ask more questions. It's their way of starting or maintaining a conversation. Men generally use questions simply to get information.

10. *Women are more intuitive than men.*
    False: There is no truth to the myth that women have a sixth sense. They are simply better "people readers." Studies have shown that baby girls are more aware of people's faces and expressions than baby boys. This carries over into adulthood and probably explains why women can often perceive a person's emotional state better than men. Have you ever heard a woman say, "I know there's something wrong; I can see it in your face"? That's good listening and reading of nonverbal signals, not "women's intuition."

11. *At business meetings, people are more likely to listen to men than women.*
    True: Male and female audiences of all sizes tend to listen more attentively to male speakers. The audiences also tend to remember more information from presentations by male speakers, even when the presentations are identical to females'. Another study showed that there is usually less noise in the room when men speak.

2

12. *Men and women laugh at the same things.*
   False: Women tell jokes less frequently, and do so more often when they are in a small, female group. Men are more likely to tell jokes in a larger, mixed-sex group, and tend to joke around with one another as a bonding technique. Male humor also tends to be more hostile, abrasive, and sarcastic than female humor.

13. *Women touch others more often.*
   False: Men are more likely to touch women when they guide them through doors, assist them with coats, and help them into cars. Linguist Nancy Henley's research shows that, in a variety of outdoor settings, men touched women four times as much as women touched men. Men also touch each other—backslapping and handshakes, for instance—more than women. Remember, too, that touching often has to do with power. A person with power touches more often than a person without.

14. *Women confront problems more directly and are more likely to bring up a problem first.*
   True: Even though men make more direct statements, a recent survey indicated that women tend to confront and bring up problems quicker and more often. Even so, women tend to be more indirect and polite, which may minimize the problem.

Chapter *Three*

Barriers to Diversity

Chapter Objectives

▶ Define *prejudice* and understand where it comes from.

▶ Define *stereotyping* and *discrimination*.

▶ Understand how prejudices affect our work and life.

▶ Define and understand *friendly fire*.

▶ Understand how nonverbal behavior can hurt relationships.

> **Diversity itself isn't a problem. The problems lie in our attitudes toward diversity.**

As we've seen, people are diverse in many ways. When we accept our differences and learn to work with them, we enrich our lives and improve the creativity and productivity of our organizations. But too often, we work against our differences and allow them to hinder instead of help us.

What are the Barriers?

Why do we have so many problems dealing with diversity? Diversity itself isn't a problem—our differences have always been there; they're what make us unique. The problems lie in our attitudes toward diversity. People who have negative attitudes toward other people's differences often engage in negative behaviors, including:

◆ Prejudice

◆ Stereotyping

◆ Discrimination

To keep these negative behaviors from becoming barriers to organizational diversity, we must learn to recognize and avoid them—in our business relationships, our treatment of employees, our hiring and firing practices, and our marketing. Prejudice, stereotyping, and discrimination hurt people—and hurt a business's bottom line.

Prejudice

Prejudice is a preconceived feeling or bias—Voltaire called it an opinion without judgment—and it's a normal human reaction. Each of us has biases of one kind or another. Some people absolutely hate cats even though they've never owned one; some people own dozens. Some people hate spinach because their parents forced them to eat it; some people think spinach makes them smarter or stronger. Some people wouldn't be caught dead driving a certain make of car or wearing certain brands of clothes; other people swear by them. We all have different likes and dislikes, and that's okay.

Prejudice is a preconceived feeling or bias.

3

Take a Moment

What are some of your likes and dislikes? How do you think you developed these biases?

_____

_____

_____

_____

Our prejudices come from our family, our friends, our environment, the media, and other external influences— wherever we first learn our beliefs. As long as our biases are about unimportant things, like our brand of toothpaste, they're relatively harmless. But when we hold prejudices against other people, we create all kinds of problems.

Prejudice against people comes from a belief in the superiority of one's own race, culture, class, or other group. It comes from believing that our own group is best or "right" and that others are not just different, but "wrong." These prejudices often lead people to create stereotypes.

Stereotyping

> **Stereotyping occurs when we apply our biases to all members of a group.**

Stereotyping occurs when we apply our biases to all members of a group. If you were raised to think that all members of a particular ethnic group are lazy, you may still hold this stereotype, no matter what your day-to-day experience tells you. If you believe strongly in this stereotype, you may also spread it to others.

We also stereotype when we apply our experiences with one member of a group to the entire group. If you met one member of a particular culture who treated you rudely, it might be hard for you to recognize that not all members of that culture are rude. But just because one member of a race, gender, age group, or culture acts a certain way doesn't mean every other person of that group will act the same way. Your perceptions could be based on a lack of knowledge because you haven't taken the time to understand the other person or culture.

Stereotypes often lead to assumptions that are insupportable and offensive. They cloud the fact that *all* attributes may be found in *all* groups and individuals. Stereotypes show up in phrases like, "What else would you expect from an intellectual?" or "Men won't ask for directions," or "All blondes are dumb."

Take a Moment

Fill in the blanks below with stereotypes you've heard:

• A real man/woman is _____.

• Americans are too _____.

• All foreigners are _____.

• Blacks/whites are too_____.

• Jews are particularly _____.

• Asians are _____.

• Gays and lesbians are_____.

3

The stereotypes we attach to people hurt us as much as they hurt everybody else, because we can't get to know the other people for who they really are. Worse still, stereotypes lead to discrimination.

Discrimination

Discrimination does not mean failing to hire enough women, minorities, or gays; it doesn't even mean refusing to associate with people from other cultures. *Discrimination* is treating people differently, unequally, and usually negatively because they are members of a particular group. We develop prejudices, turn them into stereotypes, and allow them to grow into discrimination. Prejudice can take many forms—ethnic, cultural, sexual, physical, mental, verbal—and so can discrimination—racism, sexism, heightism, weightism, ageism, anti-Semitism, religious bigotry—the list goes on and on.

Discrimination **is treating people differently, unequally, and usually negatively because they are members of a particular group.**

Take a Moment

Have you ever been discriminated against? Have you ever witnessed an incident of discrimination against another person? How did you handle it?

_____

_____

_____

Consequences for Your Organization

You have a responsibility to speak out against intolerance. If you don't, the consequences for you and your company could be staggering.

Unfortunately, prejudice, stereotyping, and discrimination are still facts of life in our society and our workplaces. We see these barriers to diversity every day in the form of racist or sexist jokes, rude remarks, or the refusal to hire or promote. If you encountered a person being discriminated against today, how would you handle it? Keep in mind that doing nothing is also taking a position. If you have friends or coworkers who are discriminatory and you accept that part of them without protest, you are actually aiding discrimination. You have a responsibility to speak out against intolerance. If you don't, the consequences for you and your company could be staggering. Consider the following statistics:

In 1994, American workers filed a record number of job bias claims—104,906—an increase of 5,000 over 1993 filings. While the overall numbers dropped in 1995, filings based on gender, disability, and religious discrimination all hit high points.

Bias Suit Filings	1993	1994	1995
Race	31,695	31,656	30,040
Gender	23,919	25,860	26,222
Age	19,884	19,571	14,649
Disability	15,274	18,859	19,798
National Origin	7,454	7,414	7,048
Religion	1,449	1,546	1,588
Totals	99,675	104,906	99,345

(Figures courtesy of the Equal Employment Opportunity Commission, June 1996.)

American business pays a price for its inability to deal successfully with diversity:

◆ Racial bias claims alone cost the American economy about $215 billion a year. That's almost 4 percent of the gross domestic product!

◆ More than one-third of the Fortune 500 companies have been sued for sexual harassment, many of them more than once. A *Working Woman* magazine survey of Fortune 500 businesses in 1988 determined that the direct costs of sexual harassment averaged $6.7 million in lost productivity, absenteeism, and turnover annually per company. One expert estimates that when overall gender bias is figured in, companies lose over $15 million per year.

◆ Age discrimination cases are up since the Age Discrimination Act went into effect in 1987, with a median of $219,000 awarded in successful suits.

◆ Disability claims have also been rising since the Americans with Disabilities Act went into effect in 1992. It's still a new law, but it's already having a major effect on the way we do business by giving the physically challenged a way to be heard.

3

> **Racial bias claims alone cost the American economy about $215 billion a year.**

◆ National origin claims peaked in 1993, but have now declined by about 6 percent. Claims of religious discrimination, however, are growing—up by nearly 10 percent in 1995 over 1993.

Besides the expense of a settlement, a discrimination claim can cost your company a tremendous amount of money in court costs and attorney fees. If a discrimination case goes to court, it can take more than three years to be heard, which adds to the expense.

Significantly, about half of all discrimination lawsuits don't make it to court. Some are settled out of court but can still be expensive for a company. Others are dismissed because they resulted from misunderstandings, miscommunication, or oversensitivity rather than malicious intent. Even lawsuits that are dismissed, however, can cost your company—in money, time, energy, and reputation—simply because of something somebody said or did unintentionally. This type of lawsuit is perhaps the most wasteful, because so many unintentional offenses can be easily prevented.

Friendly Fire

The military uses the phrase "friendly fire" to describe situations in which troops inadvertently come under fire from their comrades. I think it's an excellent way to describe those situations in which we say or do something without thinking and end up hurting someone else in an attempt to be our own friendly selves.

> **What you say is not always what they hear, and what you mean is not always what they understand.**

Friendly fire is unintentional discrimination that occurs because of habit, unconscious behavior, or just plain insensitivity. We can avoid friendly fire if we take the time to think about how our words and behavior might affect others, and if we communicate with sensitivity. Two ways friendly fire can occur include:

◆ Verbally, through biased language.

◆ Nonverbally, through inappropriate gestures, movements, and other signals.

Biased Language

Though we may not intend it, we sometimes say things that can be interpreted as racist, sexist, or offensive in some way. Some of this biased language includes:

◆ Using names and descriptions to group people for no reason.

◆ Referring to different groups of people in an unequal manner.

◆ Using the wrong name to refer to a culture or group.

◆ Misusing the name of someone from a different culture.

◆ Using inappropriate labels or terms.

3

Grouping

We sometimes use names and descriptions to group people without a purpose for doing so. You might look at me and say, "She's cute for a short person," but you would never say of someone, "She's cute for an average-height person." You've probably heard people use expressions like "handsome Jewish man," "tall black woman," "great blind pianist," or "professional male secretary." These same people would never say "handsome Baptist man," "great sighted pianist," "tall white woman," or "professional female secretary." To use the designation to refer to one group is discriminatory if you wouldn't apply the same designation to other groups.

You should be especially careful to avoid the use of gender-specific terms to distinguish men from women. Feminine terms such as *authoress, poetess, waitress, stewardess, lady lawyer*, and *lady doctor* are considered offensive by many people. So are masculine terms like male secretary and male nurse. Also be careful with the suffix *-man*. In American English, many gender-specific words have been replaced with neutral ones. *Firemen* have become *firefighters; repairmen* are *repairers;* and *policemen* are *police officers*. Though grammar traditionalists may object, most people now use "they" for nonspecific references instead of the generic "he" or the cumbersome "he or she." "If you want to invite someone, add *their* name to the list."

> **You should be especially careful to avoid the use of gender-specific terms to distinguish men from women.**

Unequal References

If we are referring to several different groups of people, we need to use language that treats each group equally. When we list ethnic backgrounds on an application, for instance, they should match in format. Can you find what's wrong with this list?

- White
- African American
- American Indian
- Mexican
- Asian
- Hispanic

You might have noticed three problems with this list. The first is the category "American Indian"; many people in this category prefer to be called Native Americans. The second problem is the division of "Hispanic" and "Mexican"—Mexicans *are* Hispanic.

A not-so-obvious problem is the term "White." All the other words are ethnic terms; white is a color. The ethnic terms for white are Anglo-Saxon, Caucasian, Anglo-American, or European American. It's true that most people use the term white loosely, but we should at least be consistent in our use of color terms versus ethnic terms in the same document. If we use white, we should also use black. And remember, the white or Caucasian category doesn't always have to be listed first.

Another example of language inequality can be found on many public rest room doors. If one door says "Men" and the other door says "Ladies," they are not equivalents. The equivalent of "Men" is "Women," and the equivalent of "Ladies" is "Gentlemen."

Take a Moment

Can you find any examples of unequal references in your workplace? How would you change them to make them equal?

_____

_____

_____

_____

Mislabeling Groups or Cultures

We risk alienating members of other cultures or groups when we refer to them by a name they would prefer not be used. Some common examples of this are *Indian* instead of *Native American, Oriental* instead of *Asian, Eskimo* instead of *Inuit.* Unfortunately, even people in the same culture or group sometimes disagree on what they would like to be called. When you're in doubt, the one sure way to learn what people prefer is to ask.

Many other types of expressions can reflect a negative attitude toward other cultures. Expressions like "culturally deprived" and "culturally disadvantaged" imply superiority of one culture over another. "Non-white" implies that white is the standard by which all others are judged—similar phrases, such as non-black or non-yellow, do not exist. "Minority" ignores the fact that people of color make up the majority of the world's population (and may make up the majority of your immediate locale).

3

Individual Names

Few things are more frustrating than hearing your name mispronounced, no matter how well-intentioned the speaker. As our workplace becomes more culturally diverse, native English speakers must learn how to deal with names from a variety of cultures. Some of these names may be difficult to spell or say. To avoid offense, always ask whether you are pronouncing and spelling the name correctly. The order of names can also be confusing. Some cultures place the surname last, some place it first, and some use no surname at all.

> **As our workplace becomes more culturally diverse, native English speakers must learn how to deal with names from a variety of cultures.**

Consider this story about a businesswoman who was meeting with prospects from Singapore. When she met them, she greeted the top man, Chong Ho Win, as Mr. Win. She addressed the second man, Tsao Hoa Chee, as Mr. Chee. In her attempts to be polite, she had missed one vital piece of cross-cultural etiquette: In Singapore (as well as Vietnam, Mien, Hmong, Cambodia, and China), family names are positioned first. She was actually calling her prospects Mr. Tom and Mr. Charlie! She should have called them Mr. Chong and Mr. Tsao. Her "friendly fire" cost her a job.

> **In Latin America, most people's surnames are a combination of the father's and mother's, with only the father's name used in conversation.**

In Latin America, most people's surnames are a combination of the father's and mother's, with only the father's name used in conversation. In most Spanish-speaking countries (Mexico included), the father's name comes first. So Victor (given name) Mendoza (father's name) Costa (mother's maiden name) is called Mr. Mendoza. But in Portuguese-speaking Brazil, it's the other way around, with the mother's name positioned first.

In Thailand, Indonesia, and Korea, names run backward—Chinese style—so that the family name comes first, given name last, and "Mr." is put with the first name. And to a Thai, it's just as important to be called by the given name as it is for Japanese to be addressed by their surnames.

Unfortunately, the Chinese order of names does not apply in all of Asia. The Taiwanese, many of whom were educated in American schools, often position their given name first. Hyun Suk Kim should be called Mr. Suk, or Hyun by his friends. In Korea, whether a man's first or last name takes "Mr." is usually determined by whether he is his father's first or second son.

> **In Korea, China, Cambodia, Hmong, Mien, and Vietnam, a woman keeps her maiden name even though she precedes it with "Mrs."**

In Korea, China, Cambodia, Hmong, Mien, and Vietnam, a woman keeps her maiden name even though she precedes it with "Mrs." So the wife of Kim Young Sam, president of Korea, is known as Mrs. Sohn Myong Suk. In America, of course, when a woman keeps her maiden name, it is usually preceded by "Ms."

People from Chile add the courtesy title to their *middle* name. People from Russia, Brazil, and South America add the courtesy title to their last names. In addition, most Americans call each other by first names, even though this is *not* acceptable to many older people. This may be hard for other cultures in our workplace to accept. In the Mexican culture, for instance, first names are *seldom* acceptable because names and titles are a source of pride, tradition, and continuity. In the Japanese culture, first names are never acceptable because only family and close friends are allowed this privilege. In some Chinese cultures, even family members must call each other by relationship terms like "Sister" and "Cousin" instead of first names.

Age also plays a part in what to call people, even in America. Many of the "older" generation still prefer the terms "Mr." and "Mrs." In some other cultures, younger people must show respect by using the terms "Aunt" and "Uncle" for older people, even if the "younger" person is 90! This tradition has been practiced in Africa for many generations, and many African Americans continue it in their homes.

In business, Asian and Middle Eastern employees may be more comfortable using a courtesy title with their manager's first name (Mrs. Kay, Mr. Jeff) than using just the first name. So it may be hard for members of some cultures to jump right in to the first-name-at-work routine.

3

Inappropriate Titles and Terms

The way we refer to other people within our companies and organizations can also be offensive to people, especially if we use terms like *boss, professional, superior,* and *subordinate.* Employees are not *subordinate* to anybody—nor are those who supervise them *superior.* Departments may have a *manager,* but in today's world, the concept of a *boss* is becoming outdated. Safer choices for describing your organizational structure include manager, supervisor, team leader, team member, assistant, or associate.

> **Employees are not *subordinate* to anybody— nor are those who supervise them *superior.***

Many other seemingly innocent terms can be considered discriminatory. Terms like *working man, mankind,* and *man on the street* imply that men are the standard by which all humans are measured, while terms like *gal* and *Girl Friday* portray women as childlike and immature. Some people find slang terms like *y'all, you guys, you'uns, you people, ma'am,* and *folks* belittling and, in some cases, racist. The term *handicapped* is offensive to many disabled people, and calling someone "Honey" or "Sweetheart" can get you labeled as sexist.

Take a Moment

Listen to the titles and terms you, your coworkers, and your supervisor use when referring to one another. Do any need to be updated?

Nonverbal Communication

Our nonverbal communication, or body language, can also be a source of friendly fire. It's true that our actions often speak louder than our words. Our unspoken messages are usually understood by our peers but may easily be misinterpreted by people from other races, genders, cultures, age groups, or economic backgrounds. Although our world is becoming smaller, we will never all share the same language, culture, or mannerisms. No gestures are universal. Worse yet, sometimes our tongues say one thing, our gestures say another thing, and our symbols (clothing, jewelry, hairstyles, facial hair, body markings) say yet another thing. Mixed signals can be very misleading to other people, especially people who come from an area where the words, gestures, or symbols mean something entirely different.

Gestures

Former President George Bush gave us a great example of nonverbal friendly fire when he was making a speech in Australia. He was trying to be friendly, and he flashed what he thought was the victory sign. Unfortunately, to Australians, the version of the victory sign he offered—with the palm inward— is an insult with vulgar overtones. It embarrassed the Australians, and it could have cost us an ally.

You and I use inappropriate gestures, too, without ever thinking about how they might affect people. We fold our arms, stand in a certain position, move our body in a way that might be considered provocative or rude, or make eye contact when we shouldn't. It's so easy to offend people without really knowing it.

The gesture that means "okay" to people born or raised in the U.S. has various meanings in other countries. To your coworker from Japan, for example, it means "money." To your business associates who grew up in France, Belgium, and Tunisia, it signals "worthless," or "zero." To those from Turkey, Greece, and Malta, it refers to homosexuality. To people who grew up in the rest of Europe and Mexico, this gesture represents an obscene or lewd comment. The crooked finger that native-born Americans use to say "Come here" is also considered obscene in many cultures. It's often the way people call prostitutes, animals, or "inferior" people! So you might offend a coworker from another culture without ever knowing why!

Movement

Something as simple as how we sit may send an unintended message. For instance, people with a European heritage are sometimes offended by the open way American men cross their legs while sitting. For your European associates, it expresses crudeness. Americans in turn suspect that European men are effeminate because of the tight way they cross their legs and the limpness of their handshakes.

Even among Americans themselves, sitting, standing, and shaking hands can easily be misunderstood or maligned. Just because a woman sits with her leg crossed over her other leg (man-style) doesn't mean she is masculine; maybe she's just comfortable. A man who has a limper handshake than others should not be labeled as feminine; perhaps he has arthritis. A woman who crosses her arms over her chest during a conversation may not be shutting you out; she could just be cold. Misunderstandings occur too often simply because another person does not stand, sit, or speak the way others do.

Personal Space

We also differ in our "comfort zones"—and getting too close to someone can become friendly fire. Have you ever walked up to someone and had him back away from you? Perhaps members of his culture don't enjoy having people that close to them, while you were raised to get up close and personal. (Americans have a comfort zone of 8 inches to 3 feet, Mexican Americans will accept closeness up to 18 inches, Japanese Americans want a distance of 3 to 6 feet.) The person you stood too close to may not even be consciously aware that conversational distance or personal space was an issue—he simply knows that he feels uncomfortable.

As always, the answer to personal space decisions should be based on the other person. If you see an associate wince when you move toward her, back up. If she looks confused or worried when you stand too far away, move in. Or, if someone else's behavior makes you uncomfortable, be honest. Tell her how you feel: "I know I've never told you this, but when you get so close to me, I feel uncomfortable. It's just the way I was raised. You don't mind if I take a step backward, do you?"

> Something as simple as how we sit may send an unintended message.

3

> Americans have a comfort zone of 8 inches to 3 feet, Mexican Americans will accept closeness up to 18 inches, Japanese Americans want a distance of 3 to 6 feet.

Eye Contact

Eye contact follows the same principle as personal space. Typically, Americans are taught that the more eye contact they give, the more power they are perceived to have. In many cultures, however (especially Asian, Mexican, Latin American, Native American, and Caribbean), less eye contact is more respectful. Many African Americans were also raised this way. Americans are sometimes confused by this when their employees, coworkers, or customers don't give them the eye contact they expect. They begin to think that something is wrong or that the other person is doing something they're ashamed of. Jumping to these conclusions can harm your relationships.

Make sure that you understand other people's culture and background before becoming suspicious of them; it can save you business and help you avoid conflict. Try to make appropriate and equal eye contact when talking to others. If you perceive that their eye contact is low and fleeting, don't stare. If you perceive that they have a strong personality and enjoy watching your face as you talk, try not to be sensitive or avert your gaze too often or too quickly.

Opening Doors

If you open a door for a woman or offer to take her coat when she arrives, and she takes offense, apologize and explain your position: "Sorry, that's just my heritage showing." But do remember not to open the door for her the next time or attempt to help her off with her wrap. Today's guideline for opening doors is not based on gender, age, or hierarchy. The rule is that whoever is in the lead opens the door and holds it for the other. As for coats, most people prefer to handle their own.

Touching

Touch is another area that causes friendly fire. People in positions of authority sometimes think they can touch employees without causing offense, yet they get upset if someone from their support team reaches out to touch them. The rule of equality says that we should not use a behavior without being willing to receive it as well. Still, any touch other than a handshake is not wise behavior in the business setting; it is too easy to misunderstand.

Shaking hands is always a polite way to greet people in America, and an occasional pat on the back is acceptable. Anything else in business is risky. (Do remember, however, that people who were raised with other cultural values may not even want to shake hands as quickly or as often. In many Asian countries, for example, body contact is considered disrespectful, so the accepted greeting is a nod or a bow and a verbal exchange. Many of your Asian coworkers still carry this belief, and even though they know better, their hearts may say that you're showing disrespect when you greet them with a firm handshake.)

Shaking hands is always a polite way to greet people in America.

3

All of these precautions may seem a little overwhelming at first, but don't panic. Avoiding friendly fire doesn't mean that you have to walk on eggs, be careful of every word you say, and never look at anybody. And it doesn't mean political correctness. (In fact, even saying "politically correct" is politically incorrect now!) Adjusting your verbal and nonverbal behavior to avoid unintentionally offending someone is simply a way to keep customers and friends, avoid lawsuits, and not hurt people.

Accepting Our Differences

We need to recognize and accept that people are different and have different areas of sensitivity. I may be terribly hurt by a word or action that you think is foolish. But see it from my point of view. If you make a joke at *my* expense, you're just being friendly. If I make a joke at *your* expense, it will burn like fire.

But if it *is* just a joke and no harm was intended, forgive and forget. Going to court or losing a job or a friend over a misunderstanding is not a good use of your rights.

Quote

Let us vow to attack intolerance and discrimination wherever they occur. Unfortunately, there are still too many places in the world where intolerance based on race, color, and creed exists. It may only be passive discrimination that isolates groups or individuals who are different, but discrimination invariably degenerates into gross violations of human rights, even crimes against humanity. Ultimately, discrimination poses a threat to international peace and security. It must be understood that intolerance is unacceptable.

Amara Essy
Former President of the
General Assembly of the United Nations

Quote

It is from numberless diverse acts of courage and belief that human history is shaped. Each time a man stands up for an ideal or acts to improve the lot of others, or strikes out against injustice, he sends forth a tiny ripple of hope. And, crossing each other from a million different centers of energy and daring, those ripples build a current that can sweep down the mightiest walls of oppression and resistance.

Robert F. Kennedy

Self-Check: Chapter 3 Review

Answers appear on pages 103 and 104.

1. Match the following terms with their definitions:
   _____ Prejudice
   _____ Stereotyping
   _____ Discrimination

   a. Treating people differently because they are members of a particular group
   b. A preconceived feeling or bias
   c. Applying our biases to all members of a group

   3

2. What is meant by "friendly fire" in this book?

   _____

   _____

   _____

   _____

3. True or False?
   Racial bias costs the U.S. economy about 4 percent of the gross domestic product each year.

4. True or False?
   A discrimination suit won't cost your company time or money unless it goes to court.

5. True or False?
   Referring to a team member as a "subordinate" is no longer acceptable in today's workplace.

Chapter *Four*

Our Changing Etiquette

Chapter Objectives

▶ Appreciate the beliefs, values, and standards of behavior of other cultures.

▶ Use proper etiquette and protocol when relating to members of these cultures.

▶ Work more effectively with the three cultures most prevalent in the U.S. workforce.

To work effectively with people from other cultures or upbringings, you need to understand them and where their ideas of right and wrong come from. That's what *culture* is: the way we were raised and the values, beliefs, and standards for behavior we internalized. These factors profoundly affect our relationships, the way we do business, and our reactions to events, circumstances, and other people.

Take a Moment

List some values that you were taught as a child:

_____

_____

Have you ever met people who had different values? If so, what was your opinion of them and/or their values?

_____

_____

Adapting to Cultural Differences

Because cultures are so diverse, values, beliefs, and standards for behavior are not universal. What is right for *you* may not be right for *me*, and what is important to a member of one culture may not be important to a member of another culture.

Independence, for example, is emphasized in American culture, so people who were raised in the U.S. are ready to leave home at an early age and may continue to move throughout their lives. Because American society is so mobile, Americans tend to jump into jobs and friendships quickly. They *need* to make friends quickly because they may not be in the same city a year from now.

More traditional cultures emphasize family and long-term relationships. People who grew up in "older" cultures (European, Asian, and others) or who were raised within those older value systems don't move around as quickly or easily. They often are born and die in the same place and take time to get to know people before accepting them as friends.

You can see how these two different approaches toward friendship could cause confusion in the workplace. A typical American might appear pushy and overly familiar to someone from a more traditional culture, while the more traditional approach to friendship might seem formal and standoffish to a typical American. Americans also tend to have different sets of friends—work friends, social friends, and neighborhood friends. Members of other cultures more often include friends in all aspects of their lives. So if you are friendly at work, they may not understand why you don't invite them to socialize. These differences could lead to misunderstandings and friendly fire, creating an unpleasant working relationship.

We all need to realize that the way we do something may not be the way someone else would do it—or want it done. Remember the New Golden Rule: "Do unto others as *they* would have you do unto *them*." If you're totally uncertain about what to do or how to behave with coworkers from other cultures, wait and see what they do, then follow suit. If you observe in a way that doesn't make the other person self-conscious, your observations

> Because cultures are so diverse, values, beliefs, and standards for behavior are not universal.

4

> We all need to realize that the way we do something may not be the way someone else would do it—or want it done.

67

can provide you with useful information about differences in etiquette and notions of proper behavior.

Here are some additional examples of ways in which typical American values and behaviors differ from those of other cultures. What would you do in the following situations?

Giving and Receiving Compliments

■ Mary likes it when someone compliments her on her clothing, so she assumes that other people also appreciate compliments. But when she complimented Yoshi on her new dress, Yoshi looked down at the floor, murmured softly, and hurried away. How should Mary interpret Yoshi's behavior?

Instead of assuming the worst, try to understand why other people react the way they do.

If Mary were following the Old Golden Rule, she might think Yoshi was being rude or unappreciative. But if she followed the New Golden Rule, she would, instead of assuming the worst, try to understand why Yoshi reacted as she did. Mary might be more understanding if she knew that many Asians believe that accepting praise in front of others is vain. Instead of praising Yoshi out loud, she could praise her in writing or quietly at her desk and not expect her to beam visibly. (She may still beam inside, however.)

Recognizing Personal Achievement

■ José had just won an important new client for his firm, yet he'd hardly mentioned his achievement. When José's manager mentioned his success during the weekly staff meeting, José seemed embarrassed and emphasized the contributions of his team members. How can José's manager recognize his accomplishment?

What would a "typical" American do if he made a major contribution to his company? He would probably talk about his accomplishment and take credit for it. Hispanic coworkers or employees might find this type of behavior rude. Traditional Hispanics believe in placing the group before the individual. Loyalty to the team and family is outranked only by loyalty to God. So a person who was raised with Hispanic values will probably defer all individual praise to the department or the team. Instead of forcing José to accept individual praise when he is clearly uncomfortable with it, José's manager could follow José's example and praise the entire team.

People raised with American values tend to be motivated by incentives, personal compliments, recognition of achievement, and increased responsibility. Mexican Americans tend to be motivated instead by managers who show personal concern for them, job security, and reduced risk. Japanese Americans tend to be motivated by security, achievement, a sense of belonging, and being part of a team.

Time

■ Mike could feel his blood pressure rising. He'd had difficulty finding a parking place and arrived five minutes late for his meeting, but his client had kept him waiting another half-hour. No one had offered him any explanation. "How much longer should I wait?" he asked himself.

4

Punctuality is highly valued by business-oriented Americans. They rush to and from everything and place a high priority on meeting deadlines. To people from other cultures and upbringings, however, including pleasure-oriented Americans, time may have less significance. Native Americans, for instance, believe that since you can't be in two places at once, you should be wherever you are needed when you are needed rather than being governed by a clock. This doesn't mean that they disregard time or schedules, it's just that they value the concept of time differently. Many Mexican Americans consider themselves punctual up to 30 minutes past the scheduled time.

> **Punctuality is highly valued by business-oriented Americans. To people from other cultures and upbringings, time may have less significance.**

How should people with different perspectives on time handle business meetings? In the case of meetings, everyone should be slightly flexible but should not be expected to wait very long. Accepted protocol says that 15 minutes is long enough to wait for an appointment. If you have somewhere else to go, or something else to do, leave a note explaining that you waited as long as you could and will reschedule as soon as possible. It should be the responsibility of the person who "stood you up" to reschedule, but that may not always happen.

Manager/Employee Relations

■ The fulfillment department was shorthanded, and Yoko was working extra hard to take up the slack. She knew they were a little behind schedule, but she couldn't believe it when her manager stood next to her and started pressing mailing labels onto boxes. "Oh, no," thought Yoko, "I must have really done something wrong."

In mainstream American culture, managers rolling up their sleeves and working beside employees is a sign of teamwork. And those managers would be astounded if this behavior were taken as a sign of anything else. Many Asians, however, were raised to interpret this behavior as an accusation that their work is not up to par. In extreme cases, an Asian employee may consider it an insult, causing loss of face. At the very least, this misunderstanding could create an instance of friendly fire. Worse, the employee might lose respect for the manager because the manager did not remain aloof. Asian employees, as well as Native Americans, would probably never discuss these feelings with their managers, because they have been taught to respect seniority in public. Managers working with different cultures should explain their motives before diving into an employee's tasks.

As you interact with people from other cultures, try to identify and respect their culture's values and standards for behavior.

As you interact with people from other cultures, try to identify and respect their culture's values and standards for behavior. If you violate the formality that many cultures prefer, the person may be temporarily offended. But if you genuinely appreciate the other person's perspective and make your error out of ignorance or forgetfulness, that person will probably sense the innocence of the error and react accordingly.

Beliefs, values, and behaviors aren't the only cultural differences that can create misunderstanding in the workplace. Language differences can also create a variety of communication problems.

Communicating with Non-Native English Speakers

Almost 9 percent of all U.S. citizens were not born in the U.S., so many workers speak English as a second or third language, and 21 percent speak no (or very poor) English. This language gap can contribute to a variety of misunderstandings.

Imagine that English is a new language for you. You understand most American words and their literal meanings, but you learned from textbooks, not from real life. What would you picture if someone told you, "After you get the hang of it, it will be a piece of cake"? or "Let's put on our thinking caps and keep our noses to the grindstone so we can whip the competition"?

In America, idioms are as common as apple pie. In fact, we often forget that idioms are meaningless phrases instead of a new wave in communication. Unfortunately, when people don't speak fluent English (and sometimes even when they do), they may have a hard time understanding idioms. Even "first thing in the morning" means different things to different people, doesn't it? And what about that old favorite, "in just a minute"? How long is a minute? It depends on whose minute it is!

If you are a native speaker of English, don't assume that someone understands you just because they speak to you in English or nod in agreement. Members of many cultures will not question you about unfamiliar words or expressions, because they believe that to do so is disrespectful, suggesting you didn't make yourself clear. They may also be afraid of appearing as though they have trouble understanding instructions. To communicate effectively with non-native English speakers, try the following techniques:

◆ Avoid jargon, slang, and idioms.

◆ Slow down your speech (but don't talk louder—hearing is not the problem).

◆ Use simple words.

◆ Pronounce and enunciate clearly.

4

Imagine that English is a new language for you. What would you picture if someone told you, "After you get the hang of it, it will be a piece of cake"?

◆ Repeat your ideas in different words.

◆ Check for understanding.

If you are a non-native English speaker, don't be afraid to ask coworkers to slow down or repeat themselves—your request will not be considered rude. If someone uses an expression that you don't understand, ask about it—your coworker will probably enjoy explaining it to you.

Using Accepted Protocol

Because members of different cultures often have very different standards for behavior, they may want to use the accepted forms of etiquette and protocol of the society in which they live and work—at least until they have discussed their cultural differences and agreed to accept them.

Self-Check: American Protocol

Let's take a quiz to make sure that you're aware of some of today's typical American protocol. Answers are given at the end of the chapter. Remember, however, that it's the spirit of etiquette that matters, not the letter.

Indicate True or False for each statement.

Socializing

_____ 1. The highest-ranking person is always mentioned first in an introduction.

_____ 2. When introducing someone, you should say that person's name before their title or relationship to you.

_____ 3. A handshake is always an acceptable greeting.

_____ 4. Politics is a good topic for small talk.

Meetings

_____ 1. When you enter someone's office for a meeting, you should always choose the chair closest to the door.

_____ 2. It doesn't matter who leaves the meeting first when it is over.

_____ 3. It's all right to just "stop by" to see business associates.

Names

_____ 1. People without an M.D. or a Ph.D. are never addressed as "Doctor."

_____ 2. People who have an earned or designated title (President, Senator, General) should still be referred to by that title even after they retire.

4

American Culture Comparison

The chart on page 74 is a guide for the three most prevalent cultures you will be working with in America. (Of course, the chart will be especially helpful if you are traveling to Mexico or Japan.) Please remember that it is only a guide. Every individual in every family in every city in every country is an individual. Remember, too, that our individual differences, such as age, style, gender, and so on, come into play in addition to our cultural and ethnic backgrounds; an older female in the U.S., Mexico, Asia, or any other area may act very differently from a younger male in the same area. If, however, you want to understand a person's cultural tendencies, or better yet, practice them when dealing with that coworker or business associate, here is a guide you can use.

Our individual differences, such as age, style, gender, and so on, come into play in addition to our cultural and ethnic backgrounds.

	NATIVE-BORN AMERICANS	MEXICAN AMERICANS	JAPANESE AMERICANS
Greeting	Usually outgoing, shake hands firmly. Socially, men may hug or kiss cheeks with women, and women may do the same with men.	Medium formality. Always shake hands (moderate grip) or give a slight bow (especially with women) in business. Tend to hold handshakes for a while and repeat frequently. Socially, friends may hug; women may kiss cheeks.	Comfortable shaking hands but will do so gently. The native way is a long, low bow instead.
Business Cards	Not automatically exchanged on meeting but always handed out if there is some reason to get in touch later. No one will refuse your card, but don't be offended if you don't get one in return.	Prefer to give cards at start of business meeting, after introductions. No particular protocol.	Prefer to exchange cards before shaking hands (or bowing). To present your card in Japanese style, use both hands, with type facing the recipient, right side up. Examine theirs, turn it over, admire it; never fold it or write on it. It is considered impolite to receive a card and not give one back.
Eye Contact	Moderate to strong.	Strong, but usually drop eyes as sign of respect.	The more respected a person, the less direct eye contact is used.
Decision-Making Style	Quickly, usually independently.	Those in authority are not expected to solicit input from colleagues, so decisions may take longer than many people are comfortable with.	By consensus, and sometimes a very time-consuming process. High-level people are seldom seen making decisions. When negotiating, will want you to come down from initial offering. Don't like to say no, but that doesn't mean yes.
Negotiating Style	Most don't worry about building relationships. Ready to get down to business, so there's little time spent on small talk before business. One-on-one, usually between high-level individuals. Informal. Ask for more than they expect. Timing is important.	Slow, indirect. Will appeal to personal relationship. Love to bargain and play with offers.	Slow, formal. Building a personal relationship comes before building a professional relationship. Usually done in a collective group. High-level people seldom speak. Will be well-informed about topic.
Problem-Solving Style	Systematically and through trial and error.	By taking the leader's vision. Careful consideration of everything. Use intuition.	With group input. Thorough.

Cooperation in the Diverse Workplace

No matter what your level of intelligence, talent, or business acumen, your success in the workplace depends to a large extent on your ability to work with other people. And now those people are multifaceted, multiracial, and multicultural.

When you adapt your behaviors to the cultural practices of others, you're more likely to earn cooperation and support, get commitments, gain friends and clients, and keep peace. The people you depend on to keep your business running—clients, coworkers, and customers—will usually come through for you.

As John Naisbitt observes in *Megatrends,* "Whenever new technology is introduced into society, there must be a counterbalancing human response." As our society becomes increasingly high-tech as well as multicultural, the need for a nonoffensive, sensitive, and personal touch in our interactions increases.

> **When you adapt your behaviors to the cultural practices of others, you're more likely to earn cooperation and support.**

4

Self-Check: Chapter 4 Review

Answers appear on page 104.

1. What is the New Golden Rule?

   _____

   _____

2. How long should you be expected to wait for a business meeting?

   _____

3. True or False?
   No matter what the culture, everyone enjoys being complimented in front of their coworkers.

4. Which of the following is *not* a good way to adapt to a non-native English speaker?
   a. Avoid jargon.
   b. Slow down your speech.
   c. Talk louder.
   d. Enunciate clearly.

5. True or False?
   Because members of different cultures often have very different standards for behavior, they may want to use the accepted forms of etiquette and protocol of the society in which they live and work.

American Protocol Quiz Answers

Socializing

1. *The highest-ranking person is always mentioned first in an introduction.* **True**

2. *When introducing someone, you should say that person's name before his or her title or relationship to you.*
   True: Most people want an identity first and a title second.

3. *A handshake is always an acceptable greeting.*
   True: Just remember that neither a bone-crushing handshake nor a "weak fish" handshake is impressive.

4. *Politics is a good topic for small talk.*
   False: Not unless you know they agree with you. Also avoid religion. Safe topics include sports, weather, locale, food, arts, and travel.

Meetings

1. *When you enter someone's office for a meeting, you should always choose the chair closest to the door.*
   False: The person who inhabits the office will most likely show you where to sit. You can ask to move, but they will direct you to where they want you to be.

2. *It doesn't matter who leaves the meeting first when it is over.*
   False: The person who called the meeting decides when it's over. This may be hard for some people to accept because in many cultures, rank and age always determine who rises, sits, and leaves first.

3. *It's all right to just "stop by" to see business associates.*
   False: Protocol mandates that we phone first.

Names

1. *People without an M.D. or a Ph.D. are never addressed as "Doctor."*
   False: In America, dentists and veterinarians are also addressed as "Doctor." But the term is not used as a sign of respect as it is in many other countries.

2. *People who have an earned or designated title (President, Senator, General) should still be referred to by that title even after they retire.* **True**

4

Chapter *Five*

Confronting Prejudice and Discrimination

Chapter Objectives

▶ Communicate more effectively.

▶ Give feedback more clearly.

▶ Confront prejudice and discrimination.

We may have an easier time responding to prejudice and discrimination if we think of ourselves as giving feedback rather than starting a confrontation.

F ew people enjoy confrontation. In fact, many of us will go out of our way to avoid it! For this reason, we may be tempted to overlook instances of prejudice and discrimination in the workplace. But when it comes to these behaviors, turning our backs can only make an unfortunate situation worse. Prejudice and discrimination create a hostile work environment that robs all employees of the energy they need to be productive. Eliminating these negative behaviors can release that energy and produce positive, constructive results.

We may have an easier time responding to prejudice and discrimination if we think of ourselves as giving feedback rather than starting a confrontation. *Feedback* is a form of communication that helps other people see their behavior as *we* see it. Feedback should not be used to criticize a *person,* only to describe what the person is *doing* and your reaction to it. If your reaction is positive, feedback can reinforce the behavior. If your reaction is negative, feedback conveys the message "I like you, but I don't like what you've done."

Is It Really Prejudice?

Before you provide feedback on behavior that you perceive to be prejudice or discrimination, analyze the situation carefully to be sure it isn't just a simple misunderstanding or friendly fire. By reviewing the situation before you speak, you have a better chance of finding the truth and not making the situation worse. Remember that people often respond differently to situations because they don't have the same:

◆ Information (knowledge each person has)

◆ Goals (what each wants to accomplish)

◆ Values (what is important to each)

◆ Methods (how something is done)

◆ Perceptions (how each sees the situation)

◆ Cultural background (maybe it's not offensive behavior where the other person comes from)

5

To further diagnose the situation, ask yourself these important questions:

◆ How important is this issue? Am I overreacting? Why am I really bringing it up?

◆ What will I gain/lose by bringing it up? What will I gain/lose by not bringing it up?

◆ Is it really prejudice or just friendly fire?

◆ How frequently do these types of situations occur with this person? Can I overlook a one-time mistake? Are others having the same problems?

◆ Am I bringing any biases or misinformation to the situation? Am I being objective?

◆ How does this person view me? Would they consider me insensitive or biased?

◆ What actions can I take to help change the situation?

◆ Am I ready and willing to make the effort to resolve it?

◆ What changes am I actually looking for?

Take a Moment

Recall a situation in which someone's words or actions made you uncomfortable. How would you deal with the same situation today?

Guidelines for Feedback

If you still feel that you have encountered prejudice or discrimination after considering these questions, approach the other person with your feedback. Use the following guidelines to increase the likelihood that your feedback is well-received and that the intent of the feedback—change in the other person's behavior—is realized:

Feedback is most helpful when given soon after the behavior occurs. Present your feedback in a private place, away from other people, and be sure emotions have cooled.

◆ **Check your timing.** Feedback is most helpful when given soon after the behavior occurs; however, it should always be appropriately timed. Present your feedback in a private place, away from other people, and be sure emotions have cooled. Check the other person's readiness by asking, "I have an issue to discuss with you. It should take about 20 minutes. Is now a good time?" or "I'd like to discuss what happened this morning. Is now a good time?" If the other person says yes, present your feedback. If the person says no, ask, "When is a good time?"

If the other person would rather discuss the issue at another time, make an appointment and arrive for it promptly. When you arrive, ask again, "Is it convenient to talk now?" If it still isn't convenient for the other person, ask again, "When will be a good time?" Stay calm and avoid any hint of exasperation or sarcasm. If you remain polite and persistent, you will eventually get your chance to speak.

◆ **State the problem as *your* problem or as a common problem.** An effective way of dealing with a negative behavior is to describe the situation from your perspective: "I'm having a problem with the joke you told this afternoon." This gives the other person an opportunity to respond without being put on the defensive.

You can also state the problem as a common problem: "Kay, there seems to be a problem with your perception of Nancy's work habits." This technique is known as *triangulation.* Often, when two people have a conflict, the situation turns into me against you. If, instead of working against each other, those involved can work against the problem, they can solve it. So instead of confronting the other person with "You have a bad attitude" or "You bigot!" try "Kay, we seem to have a problem getting along, and I'd like to talk about it. Is now a good time?"

♦ **Be empathetic.** Put yourself in the other person's shoes; acknowledge that person's needs and point of view. The major barrier to communication is our natural tendency to judge, evaluate, and approve or disapprove of others. Suppose the person next to you at lunch today says, "I really like what Kay has to say in her book," what would you say? Your reply would probably be either, "I do too!" or "I think it's terrible." In other words, your first reaction would be to evaluate your friend's statement from your point of view, and approve or disapprove of what your friend said. Although the tendency to make evaluations is common in almost all conversation, it is heightened in situations where feelings and emotions are involved. Empathy can help us listen, be more sensitive, and not judge so quickly. A sincere attempt to understand someone else's view usually makes that person more receptive to our ideas.

> The major barrier to communication is our natural tendency to judge, evaluate, and approve or disapprove of others.

Empathetic statements reflect the person's feelings, not just their words. In a heated situation, you might say, "I can see that you're angry about this" or "I can hear that you feel like you're being discriminated against" or "I can tell that my statement bothered you. Will you tell me why?"

> Feedback should address what a person did, not who that person is.

♦ **Acknowledge the other person as a unique individual.** Feedback should address what a person did, not who that person is. You're not evaluating the person, you're addressing behavior or performance. When the person expresses feelings—positive or negative—in reaction to your comments, respond with statements that indicate you understand their feelings: "I understand that you're angry about this; I might be too. But it has to be resolved."

5

◆ **Paraphrase, clarify, and ask thoughtful questions.** When you don't really understand, or if you just want to make sure you understand clearly, the best thing to do is paraphrase or clarify: "You smiled when they made that crack about Jews, but I thought I sensed anger too. Did it bother you?" or "So because you're Catholic, you feel that you shouldn't be required to work on Sundays, is that correct?"

◆ **Mirror and align with the other person.** Remember, the more you are like them, the more they will like you. You certainly don't need to try to turn into the other person, but for that particular moment, try to mirror that person's body language and align with their processing style (seeing, hearing, touching) so you are on the same wavelength.

◆ **Bring in a third party if necessary.** If you reach a point where nothing is being solved, you may want to ask an outsider for their opinion. Make sure that this other person is not biased for or against either party or the situation.

◆ **Thank the other person for their cooperation and willingness to consider changes in behavior.** Say "I appreciate your efforts to address this issue. It's been bothering me, and now I feel like we have a handle on it. I appreciate your willingness to talk about this. We still don't agree, but I'm glad we were able to discuss it."

> Following specific steps when you give feedback can help you stay on track and avoid becoming unnecessarily emotional.

Follow a Feedback Formula

Following specific steps when you give feedback can help you stay on track and avoid becoming unnecessarily emotional. The following formula incorporates the guidelines discussed above. The first letters of each step spell out D.E.A.R.—Describe, Express, Ask, and Review. This formula works best if it's used in exactly this order. Remember that the timing of feedback can also be critical, so choose an appropriate, private time and place.

The D.E.A.R. Formula

Describe the other person's behavior objectively and give specific examples (not assumptions or hearsay). Telling someone, "Your comments were inappropriate" does not explain what was unacceptable to you. What were the comments? What about them was inappropriate? Why?

Here are some clear descriptions of behavior that could be used to begin a feedback session:

1. "When I'm referred to as a 'girl,' as I was at today's meeting . . ."

2. "When people touch my hair, as you did this morning . . ."

3. "When racist humor is perpetuated, like the joke you used in this week's column . . ."

4. "Your use of the word (derogatory term) . . ."

(We'll complete these sentences in our next set of examples.)

Express how you feel and explain the effect the behavior or situation had on you, the rest of the group, or another person. Explain more if you wish, then pause so the other person has a chance to respond. Remember that the feedback you're providing is a description of your perception and is not absolute, even if it is important. Use "I" language (I think, I feel, I get) to describe your feelings—statements that begin with "you" tend to imply absolutes and may seem judgmental. Instead of saying, "You insensitive, sexist idiot!" try "When I see lewd pictures in your office, I feel ashamed and embarrassed."

Here are some expressions of feelings that could be used to complete the examples given above:

1. " . . . I get really frustrated. It makes me feel like you just don't care about me as a person."

2. " . . . I really dislike it. It takes hours to get it done like this, and it's very personal space."

3. " . . . it embarrasses everyone in the group."

4. " . . . is offensive and embarrassing to me and the entire department."

5

> **Remember that the feedback you're providing is a description of your perception and is not absolute, even if it is important.**

Negotiate and compromise if possible.

Ask for the other person's help and talk about the situation. Negotiate and compromise if possible. If the other person does not want to change, ask for what you want, and be sure to describe the benefit to them.

These sentences correspond to our previous examples:

1. "I'd really like to prevent this from happening again. What will it take?" (Negotiate, compromise.) "I'll tell you what. If you'll agree to call me an 'assistant' instead of a 'girl,' I'll try not to become so defensive when you forget. That should make both of our lives easier. OK?"

2. "I'll answer any questions you have about the process. Just please promise not to do it again."

3. "If you try to be a little more sensitive to everyone's feelings, I think we can work together much better."

4. "If you'll agree not to let this happen again, I'll withdraw the complaint I made to management so your name will be cleared."

Review the new agreement, then stop, as in these conclusions to our previous examples.

1. "So we've agreed that . . . "

2. "Now that you know how I feel about people touching my hair, I'm sure it won't happen again."

3. "If you find that you can't avoid using racial qualifiers in your article, you'll let me know ahead of time. Is that agreeable?"

4. "You've promised not to use terms like that at work (or around me)."

Take a Moment

Think of a situation that you need to address with someone and fill in the formula below:

Describe: "When (this behavior) happens . . . "

_____

_____

_____

"Like (when/what) . . . "

_____

_____

_____

Express Effect: "I feel . . . " or "It causes . . . "

_____

_____

_____

Ask: "How can we change this situation?" or
"What can I/we do to keep this from happening
again?"

Listen, discuss, compromise: Don't forget to be clear
about what outcome you want.

Review: "So we've agreed that . . . "

_____

_____

_____

5

What If That Doesn't Work?

What if someone makes a promise to change a behavior and doesn't? Here's another formula you can use to point out a discrepancy between somebody's words and deeds—to remind them that they agreed to act differently toward you or another person. As with the previous formula, you can use this to help keep your emotions in check and objectively describe what the other person said they would do, what they actually did, and what you want or how you feel. The steps are similar to those in the D.E.A.R. formula:

1. Agreement—Describe what they said they would do:
   - "Last week, you agreed to stop interrupting me and discrediting my input at company meetings."

2. How broken—Describe what they really did:
   - "Then today you made fun of my ideas about the new project. I'll admit that you didn't interrupt, but when you roll your eyes as though nothing I say is valuable, it has the same effect."

3. Advice—Determine what you can do about the situation. (Optional)
   - "What else can I do to get your respect?" *Talk, negotiate, compromise.*

4. Desire or incentive—State what you want or what you'll offer:
   - "How about this? If you'll just hold your tongue and not make faces while I'm speaking, I'll ask your opinion in the group when I'm finished, and you can say out loud whatever it is you're thinking. I can handle the spoken criticism, just not the nonverbal antics in the middle of my thoughts. Is that a deal?"

5. New agreement—Restate the desired outcome:
   - "So we've agreed that you'll listen calmly to my ideas until I've finished. Is that correct?"

Take a Moment

Think of a situation in which someone has not lived up to promises made to you, and fill in the formula below:

1. Agreement:

_____

_____

_____

2. How broken:

_____

_____

_____

3. Advice: ***Talk, negotiate, compromise.*** Don't forget to be clear about what outcome you want.

4. Desire or incentive:

_____

_____

_____

5. New agreement:

_____

_____

_____

5

Quote

Americans do not care as much about differences in culture or even in color (despite much rancid history under that heading) as they care about character as it is expressed in behavior. The American challenge now is not to pay homage to every cultural variation and appease every ethnic sensitivity, but rather to encourage universally accepted ideals of behavior: self-discipline, compassion, responsibility, friendship, work, courage, perseverance, honesty, loyalty, and faith.

William J. Bennett
Former Director of the
Federal Office of Drug Control Policy

Handling Touchy Situations

I did a "relationships analysis" for a large company last year. One of the questions was, "Describe your manager." A participant responded, "He is very hard to describe. Let's just say that there are more than 200 million people in the world, and he gets along with three of them." Isn't that a perfect definition of a "difficult" person?

Providing feedback about prejudice or discrimination to a difficult or sensitive person can be a special challenge.

Providing feedback about prejudice or discrimination to a difficult or sensitive person can be a special challenge. Here are some approaches for handling those touchy situations. I call this first set of phrases "escape routes." They are a way for either side to get out of the conversation and still save face. They include phrases such as:

◆ "I'm sure you're not aware of this, Gary, but . . ."

◆ "I know you don't mean to be offensive, but . . ."

◆ "Adam, we seem to have a problem . . ."

◆ "Betty, I have a problem, and I need your help."

◆ "Is now a good time for us to talk?"

◆ "I hope you don't mind my asking . . ."

◆ "I feel uncomfortable bringing this up, but . . ."

You might say, "I'm sure you're not aware of this, Gary, but when you say my clothing is unprofessional, it makes me angry. My clothing is part of my culture, and I'm proud of it." The escape route gives Gary a chance to say, "You're right. I wasn't aware of that." Gary can then apologize or ask questions. Most people will take the escape route if you offer it to them rather than fight in public.

As your interaction progresses, you can paraphrase and clarify the other person's intent and meaning with these "power phrases." They include phrases such as:

- "It appears that you feel . . ."

- "So from your point of view . . ."

- "So it seems to you . . ."

- "So from where you stand . . ."

- "It looks like you see it as . . ."

- "So you think . . ."

- "What I hear you saying is . . ."

- "It sounds like you're (angry/sad/overjoyed)."

Here are two more techniques that will help you in touchy situations:

- **Repetition:** If a person refuses to acknowledge your point of view, calmly repeat what you want or believe until you receive a response. One caution—don't let this type of situation become a yes/no, yes/no battle.

Supervisor:	I really don't think you can do this assignment.
Employee:	I know you don't, but I do think I can, and I'd like a chance to try.
Supervisor:	Well, you'll never be able to pull it off.
Employee:	I understand your opinion, but I think I can, and I'd like a chance to try.

5

> If a person refuses to acknowledge your point of view, calmly repeat what you want or believe until you receive a response.

Acknowledge criticism or offensive remarks without admitting or denying them, or becoming defensive.

◆ **Acknowledgment:** Acknowledge criticism or offensive remarks without admitting or denying them, or becoming defensive. A simple "thank you" usually works to destroy this kind of interaction too.

Employee 1: That's the ugliest "costume" I've ever seen.

Employee 2: (Don't take offense to or correct the sarcastic use of "costume," just acknowledge the remark.) I can see why you wouldn't wear it.

Employee 1: Darn right, nobody in their right mind would wear it.

Employee 2: That may be true, but I'm not just anybody.

Some Additional Guidelines

The more you give people what they need, the more they will give you what you need.

1. Check your timing before asking to talk.

2. Listen, listen, listen.

3. Listen for the unspoken too.

4. Never assume anything.

5. Remember that the more you give people what they need, the more they will give you what you need.

6. Never expect the same reaction to a statement or situation that you would have.

7. Don't be surprised at anything that comes up.

8. Don't look for praise for yourself or others.

9. Don't shame or blame anyone.

10. Allow plenty of time for the conversation.

11. Be assertive but not aggressive.

12. Remember that others may take more time to adjust than you expect.

13. Make appropriate eye contact.

14. Don't belittle or put down people's ideas or comments.

15. Never interrupt or "yes, but" people.

16. Don't tell others how they feel or what they think (now or in the future).

17. Don't compare people to other people, even yourself.

18. Be empathetic and positive.

19. Discuss points from logic, not from emotion.

20. Don't make promises you can't keep.

Stand Up for Your Rights

The thought of confronting instances of prejudice and discrimination can be intimidating. But if you think before you speak and follow a formula for providing feedback, you can improve your chances of being effective.

Everyone has a responsibility to combat prejudice and discrimination in the workplace and the community. The following communication reminders can help motivate you to work to eliminate these negative behaviors.

5

Everyone has a responsibility to combat prejudice and discrimination in the workplace and the community.

Communication Reminders

1. Everyone has a natural right to courtesy and respect.

2. By standing up for our rights, we show that we respect ourselves, and we earn respect from other people.

3. Sacrificing our rights usually results in allowing other people to mistreat us.

4. By trying to avoid conflict, we can hurt ourselves and others.

5. We decide what's important to us; we do not have to bend to other people's issues.

6. When we do what we think is right for us, we feel better about ourselves and have more authentic and satisfying relationships.

7. We all have a right to express ourselves, as long as we don't violate the rights of others.

8. It is not essential that you be loved or approved of by everyone.

9. You do not have to be perfectly competent, adequate, and successful to consider yourself worthwhile.

10. Unhappiness is seldom caused by outside circumstances and past events.

11. It is never better to avoid difficulties and responsibilities than to face them.

12. There is not always a solution to every problem.

13. In honest communication, there is no "right and wrong," just "different."

Self-Check: Chapter 5 Review

Answers appear on page 104.

1. We may have an easier time responding to prejudice or discrimination if we think of ourselves as
   _____ instead of starting a confrontation.

2. Before we confront behavior that we perceive as prejudice or discrimination, we should always _____

   _____

3. The D.E.A.R. formula stands for:

   D _____

   E _____

   A _____

   R _____

4. What are the five steps of the formula you can use to deal with situations when someone breaks a promise to change behavior?

   a. _____

   b. _____

   c. _____

   d. _____

   e. _____

5. What does the repetition technique for dealing with touchy situations involve?

   _____

   _____

5

Chapter *Six*

What Else Can You Do?

Chapter Objectives

▶ Recognize and change possibly offensive behavior.

▶ Project an attitude of caring for others.

▶ Create a plan for continued improvement.

Working effectively with diversity means recognizing the many types of differences in yourself and others. It means capitalizing on each other's strengths and compensating for each other's weaknesses. It means being appropriately assertive, saying what you mean, and asking for what you want. It means developing patience and tolerance, and handling conflict and feedback appropriately. Here are some other specific guidelines to help you manage your diverse relationships.

> Working effectively with diversity means recognizing the many types of differences in yourself and others.

Guidelines for Managing Your Diverse Relationships

Guidelines for Individuals

1. **Be aware of the change that's taking place around you, and welcome that change.**
   If we were to continue living as we have been for the last 50 or 100 years, our society would fall apart—as others have without growth. You can create your own future by creating your own change.

2. **Recognize and respect others and their individuality.**
   In a free country, each of us has the right to be ourselves (as long as we don't harm or diminish others), and that diversity is wonderful. No one has the right to impose their ideas, ideals, or values on others.

3. **Think before you speak, and be sensitive to others.**
   If you do accidentally offend someone, apologize immediately. To avoid embarrassing you, some people may deny that they felt offended. Even so, your apology will have been heard and silently appreciated.

4. **Talk about your differences and ask tactful questions about how people want to be treated:**
   "Do you mind telling me . . . ?" or "How do you feel about . . . ?" or "I'd really love to know more about . . . "

I've asked a lot of these questions in my career, and I've never had anyone take offense. Most of the time, they say, "I'm glad you asked rather than calling me something I don't want to be called or talking about me behind my back."

Quote

Formula for Handling People:

(1) Listen to the other person's story.
(2) Listen to the other person's full story.
(3) Listen to the other person's full story first.

Gen. George Marshall
Former U.S. Secretary of Defense
and Nobel Peace Prize Winner

6

If someone does object to answering your questions, however, respect that decision. Some issues are too private or painful to talk about. By giving people an option to not answer your question, you can create a sense of respect and erase any fear that may exist. This results in trust and security—a positive climate.

5. **Listen more.**
   Being listened to increases a person's self-esteem and confidence. People who are listened to usually appreciate the person who is doing the listening and are more likely to cooperate with that person. Listening encourages people to

be less defensive and to talk through concerns and solve problems. Careful listening can teach us a great deal about others' thought patterns, belief systems, values, and desires.

6. **Recognize your own biases and prejudices.**
   Prejudice is a natural human emotion. You don't have to like or agree with everyone, but you do have to treat each person with respect and equality. What you *think* is your business—what you *do* concerns others.

7. **Eliminate stereotypes and generalizations.**
   You can't understand an entire culture based on the limited amount you know about a few people. Even people who share the same culture and background are not necessarily the same. Each of us is made up of many factors. We may act one way in one role, but if you put us in a different role or add another factor, we may act another way.

   Avoid using words, images, and situations that suggest that all or most members of a particular group are the same, and identify people by race, gender, or ethnic origin only when those facts are relevant.

8. **Expose yourself to other cultures.**
   Go to an ethnic neighborhood and see what goes on. Go to another religion's place of worship and see what they do. Go out to dinner with people from other cultures and eat what they eat. At the very least, read books, see movies, or look at almanacs. Most of us prefer to be around people who are like us, but we can't grow much that way. The best way for us to grow individually is to learn about other ways of doing things.

9. **Remember that your race/gender/personality style is not the center of the universe.**
   Everyone is different. Respect people for who they are, and don't try to turn them into you. It's also important to remember that you are different too.

10. **Be careful with humor.**
    Sometimes people are so eager to put their personality into their conversations that they forget to consider how off-the-wall comments or jokes might hurt others. Off-color, sexist, religious, political, or ethnic remarks are bound to offend

someone. When they do, that person won't hear another word you say and might create trouble for you later. Your communication should meet the standards observed by educated people in careful conversation. Communication that falls below these standards only decreases your listeners' attention, hinders the relationship process, and makes you look unprofessional.

11. **Lighten up!**

Don't take everything so seriously. Who cares what color a cookie is and whether the black or white part is on the top? Whether a wine is "old" or "vintage challenged," it has still been around for a while. Whether Rover is a "dog" or a "canine life companion," he still barks at intruders. We wouldn't feel so threatened by diversity if we allowed ourselves to chuckle at our own—and others'—shortcomings.

Recognize people's *intentions,* even if they step on their own feet—or yours. Most people really don't mean to hurt others. If they *intended* to hurt you, do something about it; if they didn't, forgive them for it. If you pull on a willow branch, it bends. If you pull on an elm, it stands firm. There are times to be a willow and times to be an elm. Make sure you know which is which.

6

Take a Moment

Complete these final exercises to help you develop a plan to manage your diverse relationships better. On the first line, list the name of a person who is different from you in some way. Then think about how you and this person can have a better working relationship. After you've analyzed one relationship, try a few more!

Person's name:_____

_____

Person's strengths:_____

_____

_____

What stresses or annoys this person:

_____

_____

How this person's diversity contributes to our relationship:

_____

_____

How my diversity contributes to our relationship:

_____

_____

How I can help our relationship:

_____

_____

Plan
List five goals for changes you want to make or behaviors you want to institute concerning diversity in your organization:

_____

_____

_____

_____

_____

Guidelines for Organizations

Your organization has met EEOC requirements. You regularly hire and promote female and minority employees. You've remodeled your office to accommodate the physically challenged, installed Braille guides in your elevators, and placed amplifiers on your phones. You've cautioned everyone to avoid biased language. Are you "diversity perfect"? No, you're just beginning.

Discrimination in our country will end only with awareness of how others perceive our actions. Managing diversity well means addressing the needs of every segment of our population. It means enabling every worker to perform at his or her highest potential. It means raising awareness, teaching employees about differences and similarities, and giving them the skills to act and think differently. When we do it right, people will not be advantaged or disadvantaged because of their differences.

> Discrimination in our country will end only with awareness of how others perceive our actions.

What organizations fear, of course, is a lowering of standards, a "quota" system in which the best person doesn't necessarily win. We can't allow that to happen. Because of increased competition, quality and competence count now more than ever. The goal is to manage diversity in a way that will allow us to maintain the same productivity and quality we once achieved from a less diverse workforce. But we must learn to do so without discrimination.

6

Here are some things you can do to help your organization meet its diversity goals:

1. **Be a role model, regardless of your job title or level in the organization.**
    You can't expect other employees to adhere to humanistic behaviors and attitudes if you let incidents pass without confronting them or indicate that you secretly agree with disruptive behavior. If you don't interrupt and discredit discrimination, you're contributing to it. Emphatically state (and uphold) that issues of human dignity, justice, and safety are nonnegotiable.

> Be a role model, regardless of your job title or level in the organization.

2. **Celebrate all holidays or no holidays.**
   If you put up a Christmas tree, consider also recognizing
   Mexican Independence Day, Laotian New Year, Tet,
   Passover, Kwanzaa, and other cultural holidays.

3. **Use nonprejudicial words in your marketing and service
   efforts.** Also, make sure that all races, genders, sizes, and
   physical conditions are represented in your marketing
   materials. What kinds of people are shown in your annual
   report? your newspaper advertising? your TV spots? Is your
   marketing truly representative of diverse people, or are you
   still holding up the American ideal of able-bodied, thin,
   white, and gorgeous?

4. **Hire people who are bilingual, and advertise that you speak
   other languages.**

5. **Offer ongoing diversity training for your employees—
   at all levels.**
   Incorporate training programs that teach diversity awareness,
   perception, relationship-building, communication, and
   teamwork. All workers need an understanding of diversity
   and how it affects communication, and they need more than
   an hour's overview or a pamphlet to achieve it.

6. **Adhere to all ADA and EEOC regulations.**
   You're only paying lip service until you install enough
   wheelchair ramps and telephone amplifiers and offer classes
   for the specially abled.

7. **Check your pulse:**

   ◆ Even after all the women in your company are called
     "Ms.," and "he" has been deleted from your vocabulary,
     are the women still making 65 cents for every dollar
     earned by the men?

   ◆ Are blacks and Hispanics still working at administrative
     and service jobs, or is your management staff also
     diverse?

   ◆ Does your employee population fail to mirror the
     population percentages outlined in this book and by the
     Census Bureau?

◆ Do your programs, policies, principles, and wages give special consideration to any one group?

If you answered yes to any of the above questions, you're not managing diversity yet. The goal is not to bring minorities and women into a dominant white male culture and teach them how to get along; the goal is to create a dominant heterogeneous culture.

Take a Moment

Identify problems (and solutions) that diversity might cause in your organization:

_____

_____

_____

_____

_____

_____

Identify a plan to prevent or handle these problems:

_____

_____

_____

_____

_____

6

Conclusion

We will be stronger as people, as companies, and as a nation when we can work together, maximizing the abilities of all of our workers and putting aside racism, sexism, and all those other "isms" that separate us. In short, we will have succeeded in managing diversity when we can live up to the values set out in our Constitution. I commend you for taking the first step by reading this book and challenge you to take diversity to its full potential within yourself and your organization.

Quote

The greatest challenge America faces in the era beyond peace is to learn the art of national unity in the absence of war or some other explicit external threat. If we fail to meet that challenge, our diversity—long a source of strength—will become a destructive force. Our individuality—long our most distinctive characteristic—will be the seed of our collapse. Our freedom—long our most cherished possession—will exist only in history books.

Richard Nixon
37th President of the United States

Chapter 1

1. Differences in people

2. Less than 15 percent

3. Strength

4. Vegetable soup

5. False—By 2050, the average U.S. resident will trace his or her descent to such countries as Africa, Asia, the Hispanic countries, the Pacific Islands, and Arabia.

Chapter 2

1. False—Diversity consists of many different factors.

2. Seers (visual), Hearers (auditory), and Feelers (kinesthetic)

3. True—You should try to adjust your assertiveness level to the level of others.

4. Bulldog—d; Retriever—a; Spaniel—c; Collie—b

5. Money; rewards

6. False—Men and women don't behave in virtually the same way.

7. True—African Americans, Hispanics, Asians, and Pacific Islanders make up a little more than one quarter of the U.S. population.

Chapter 3

1. Prejudice—b; Stereotyping—c; Discrimination—a

2. Situations in which we say or do something without thinking and end up hurting someone else.

3. True—Racial bias costs the U.S. economy about 4 percent of the gross domestic product each year.

4. False—A discrimination suit will cost your company money in legal fees and lost productivity whether it goes to court or not.

5. True—More acceptable terms include "team member" or "associate."

Chapter 4

1. Do unto others as they would have you do unto them.

2. No more than 15 minutes.

3. False—Members of some cultures dislike being complimented in front of others.

4. c. Talk louder.

5. True—Adapting to the culture in which you live and work can be an effective way for members of different cultures to work together, at least until they've had time to discuss their differences.

Chapter 5

1. Providing feedback.

2. Carefully analyze the situation to be sure it isn't just a misunderstanding.

3. Describe, Express effect, Ask, Review

4. a. Agreement—Describe what they said they would do.
    b. How broken—Describe what they did.
    c. Advice—Determine what you can do about the situation.
    d. Desire or Incentive—State what you want or what you'll offer.
    e. New agreement—Restate the desired outcome.

5. Calmly repeat what you want or believe until you receive a response.